SHIFTING TIDES IN GLOBAL HIGHER EDUCATION

A.C. (Tina) Besley, Michael A. Peters,
Cameron McCarthy, Fazal Rizvi
General Editors

Vol. 9

The Global Studies in Education series is part of the Peter Lang Education list.
Every volume is peer reviewed and meets
the highest quality standards for content and production.

PETER LANG
New York • Washington, D.C./Baltimore • Bern
Frankfurt • Berlin • Brussels • Vienna • Oxford

MARY ALLISON WITT

SHIFTING TIDES IN GLOBAL HIGHER EDUCATION

Agency, Autonomy, and Governance in the Global Network

PETER LANG
New York • Washington, D.C./Baltimore • Bern
Frankfurt • Berlin • Brussels • Vienna • Oxford

Library of Congress Cataloging-in-Publication Data
Witt, Mary Allison.
Shifting tides in global higher education: agency, autonomy,
and governance in the global network / Mary Allison Witt.
p. cm. — (Global studies in education; v. 9)
Includes bibliographical references.
1. University cooperation. 2. Education, Higher—Economic aspects.
3. Education and globalization. 4. International cooperation.
I. Witt, Mary Allison.
LB2331.5.S55   378.1'04—dc22   2011006371
ISBN 978-1-4331-1468-7 (hardcover)
ISBN 978-1-4331-1467-0 (paperback)
ISSN 2153-330X

Bibliographic information published by **Die Deutsche Nationalbibliothek**.
Die Deutsche Nationalbibliothek lists this publication in the "Deutsche
Nationalbibliografie"; detailed bibliographic data is available
on the Internet at http://dnb.d-nb.de/.

The paper in this book meets the guidelines for permanence and durability
of the Committee on Production Guidelines for Book Longevity
of the Council of Library Resources.

© 2011 Peter Lang Publishing, Inc., New York
29 Broadway, 18th floor, New York, NY 10006
www.peterlang.com

All rights reserved.
Reprint or reproduction, even partially, in all forms such as microfilm,
xerography, microfiche, microcard, and offset strictly prohibited.

Printed in the United States of America

For Emmeline and Liam

Contents

Foreword ix
Acknowledgments xiii

Chapter 1 Introduction 1
   Purpose of the Research 5
   Research Questions 7
   Significance of the Research 9
   Plan for the Book 9
   Notes 12

Chapter 2 Agency and Power within Global Networks 13
   Introduction 13
   Globalization as Connectivity 14
   Agency and Power within Global Networks 19
   Local Agency and Globalization 25
   Conclusion 27

Chapter 3 Local Context in Global Flows 29
   Introduction 29
   Conceptions of Internationalization and Globalization in Higher
      Education 30
   Global Patterns of Development of International Programs 32
   National Context of the Study 40
   US Higher Education's Cultural Framing 40
   Development of US International Programs within the Global
      Marketplace 44
   Singapore's Higher Education Cultural Framing 51
   Conclusion 59
   Notes 60

Chapter 4 Methodological Challenges in a Cross-cultural Study 61
   Theoretical Rationale for Qualitative Methods 62
   Methods: Research Design 65
   Research Setting 65
   Interviews 67

Documents 69
Data Analysis 70
Conclusion 70

Chapter 5 Building a Global Alliance 71
Introduction 71
The Original Context of the Partnership, Midwestern University 73
The Original Context of the Program, Singapore University 78
Development of the Joint Master's Degree 83
Conclusion 89
Notes 90

Chapter 6 Barriers to Global Flows in Higher Education 91
Mediating Organizational Structures and Processes 93
Equivalency through Evaluation and Accreditation 95
Differences in Research and Institutional Culture 98
Stepping towards the Joint PhD 99
Negotiating Intellectual Property 103
Approval of the Multi-institutional Degree 106
The Existence Proof 108
Conclusion 112

Chapter 7 The Existence Proof 115
Introduction 115
Main Findings and Implications 115
Considerations for Further Research 128
Conclusion 129

Bibliography 133

Foreword

Many complain that bringing about change in higher education is more challenging than moving a graveyard. Whatever the metaphor, academic institutions around the globe are more likely to be known for stability and continuity than agility and sudden transformation. Governments come and go; corporations thrive and crumble; but great universities around the world somehow survive.

Still, change in higher education is constant and at times transformative: changes in curriculum and in what is judged important and worthy of study; evolution in institutional character and governance; migration and expansion of mission; alteration of the relationship between higher education institutions and the society; and changes in who pays and benefits from higher education.

In the United States whole new institutional forms have emerged, including the national network of public Land-grant universities and community colleges that took root during the last century and blossomed after World War II. More recently, we have witnessed the emergence of for-profit providers of higher education, now the most rapidly growing segment of American higher education. In Europe, Asia and Africa the changes have been no less dramatic.

Similarly, the international, transnational dimension of higher education has a rich history that has evolved and changed over time. In a real sense, knowledge and the scholars who create and nurture it know no boundaries. While graduate students from around the world tend to migrate to U.S. universities for advanced study at this moment, young scholars from America nurtured their academic careers at European universities for much of the prior century. Technology now enables medical students and scholars in multiple settings to confer on and execute complex procedures without reference to geography or national sovereignty. Understanding other languages and cultures has always been an important element but never has the interest and activity been more intense than now.

As Witt illustrates in this powerful case study, however, collaborating across institutional boundaries – as common and crucial as it is – and harmonizing institutional policies, cultures and incentives in ways that overcome the barriers to collaboration and yield the rewards initially envisioned by the partners, is incredibly complex. Often the impetus for collaboration is quite different. One partner may envision one opportunity; the other may seek a quite different incentive. Cultures and traditions – even in a time of globalization and harmonization – remain distinctive in ways the principles themselves may not understand at the inception of the joint venture. Sheer capacity may limit execution as good intentions and shared visions and values are overrun by the practical frustration of resource limits, be they financial, human, and technological or governance related. Moreover, the desire for power (or agency), a quest for autonomy and independence, and the tensions and conflicts among different traditions and cultures that shape decisions and choices – together these make the challenge of academic collaboration formidable, even across departmental boundaries, let alone across national boundaries and transnational joint ventures.

Barriers aside, globalization has transformed higher education worldwide just as it has transformed virtually every sector of the global village – business and commerce, politics, entertainment, values and belief systems and the culture itself. Knowledge is sought after, pursued and shared, often oblivious to institutional and national boundaries.

Collaboration among scholars and institutions around the globe has escalated in part because of contemporary information technology and the exponential growth in capacity to move and share information rapidly, conveniently and relatively inexpensively. These forces have changed the ways in which scholars think and work, making geography and national boundaries a less material barrier to collaboration and joint ventures.

We have much to learn from this new world. The opportunities and possibilities presented in this particular case are novel and the incentives and motives compatible and attractive. The context is an international multi-institutional graduate degree program in engineering involving two quite different academic institutions located in two quite different parts of the globe. Witt examines the phenomenon of a global network within the context of two institutional-specific nodes involving two research universities. The

saga probes the motives and desires of the partners and the ways in
which they complement and clash. As the case unfolds, we learn the significance of the cultural differences that facilitate and impede collaboration and explore the adaptations of the two quite different governance and decision-making traditions.

What does Witt's case study tell us?

- By the very nature of the case itself, we understand that global collaboration has moved well beyond earlier notions of international academic programs involving the movement of students and faculty members. In this case, joint academic degree programs of graduate education and sophisticated research initiatives were at the heart of the joint venture.
- We also learn that quite different motives can nonetheless be compatible and mutually reinforcing. In the case of the U.S. Midwest research university, the incentives involved a prominent global presence and footprint; research and innovation opportunities; and some potential financial reward. For the Singapore government the collaboration fit nicely into a larger long range strategic vision. For Singaporean students, the degree program offered many (although far from all) of the advantages of a major U.S. research university.
- The facts of the case suggest that power relationships between and among faculties and institutions defy stereotype. Flows of power and initiative were multi-directional and often unpredictable.
- Happily, at least to this reader, is the reassurance that higher education is not able to bend the culture to work its will, but is transformed and adapted to the specific Singaporean culture.

Higher education institutions and programs are changing around the world in response to evolving fields of knowledge, altered government/social policies and priorities, changing economic forces, empowering technological developments, new student preferences and countless other forces. One can not foresee the future, but the reality of a larger but yet more accessible and interdependent global village is growing ever more obvious. Since knowledge knows no boundary, information and human beings can and will move rapidly in response to competition, opportunity and whim.

The shifting tides of globalization in higher education will not soon recede. Universities and colleges must learn to live and thrive in this new environment. While only one instance, a mere single case, this study of global collaboration is one from which all of higher education can learn.

Stanley O. Ikenberry

Acknowledgments

I would like to extend my warmest appreciation to the participants of this study at both sites who so graciously gave of their time and who hosted me so kindly during my research at their campuses. I owe a particular debt of gratitude to Professor Fazal Rizvi, who guided the project and offered invaluable counsel throughout the development of this book. In addition, I am indebted to Professor Michael Peters for his assistance and support throughout this project. I am also grateful to President Emeritus Stanley O. Ikenberry and Dean Mary Kalantzis of the University of Illinois, who offered guidance through the long writing and research process and arranged their arduous schedules to assist me. Their dedication is further evidence that despite numerous global, market, funding and other pressures, a student's education remains top priority at large US Land-grant institutions.

I am thankful to friends and family who encouraged my progress, particularly Tysza Ghanda, who listened, counseled and read drafts. I am grateful to colleagues at the Illinois Board of Higher Education for the vibrant and supportive environment which bolstered me while the book was in the final editing process. I am very grateful to my children for patiently allowing me to do this work. Finally, immeasurable gratitude is due to Steve Witt for all sorts of things too numerous to mention.

CHAPTER ONE

Introduction

In early 2008, the largest fleet of ships ever assembled in the history of the globe lay in wait in the Singapore harbor. Not an invading army, but instead, empty container vessels waiting for cargo that had not come. Day after day, the enormous vessels sat, hulls stretched to the sky without the ballast of freight, marooned on the lagging tide of the global economy. In other harbors around the world, ships were idle as well, with around 150 waiting in the Straits of Gibraltar, 300 around Rotterdam, yet Singapore, close to Asian markets attracted by far the highest number, over 735 (Bradsher, 2009). If a rising tide lifts all boats, then this empty armada exemplifies what happens when the global economic tide recedes.

By now, the theories of globalization are well traveled channels in academic literature. Multiple routes have been charted through this "no man's land" (Bauman, 1998), and the contested term "globalization" is written about from many different perspectives. Discussions about globalization debate not only its definition, but also its beginnings and consequences. As Rizvi and Lingard have summarized,

> These debates focus on such questions as how globalization should be measured; what is its chronology; what are its causes; how might we explain the ways in which globalization contributes to various economic, social and cultural transformations; and . . . what are its implications for public policy. (2010, p. 23)

According to Held, globalization is first and foremost a stretching of social, political, and economic activities across borders to such an extent that events, decisions and activities in one region of the world come to have significance in distant regions of the globe. In this sense, the term embodies transregional interconnectedness, including the widening reach of networked power (2003, p. 67).

Within the concept of transregional interconnectedness, a number of discussions are ongoing, examining globalization using a variety of lenses. Divisions exist between those who see economic forces as the determining feature of global networks and those who posit economic, political and cultural levels as structurally overlapping or independent. The efficacy and effects of neoliberalism and its dedication to free market individualism, private property, constitutional order, and a minimal state continue to dominate much of the debate about global networks. For some, contemporary globalization represents the fact that American capitalism disseminated neoliberalism across the planet, reshaping policy agendas in many countries. In some interpretations, globalization *is* neoliberalism. Others cite "globalization from below" as resistance to neoliberal pressures. Yet in each of those examples, the globally networked power of neoliberalism remains a central tenet.

Of course, as Deem (2001) as well as Pierson (1998) have pointed out, the effects of globalization need to be considered somewhat cautiously. Both proponents of globalization theories (Held, 2003) and critics (Hirst, 1996) have noted that some claims for globalization and its effects are either exaggerated or not well substantiated.

Networks and flows have become familiar images among the dominant characterizations of globalization as Marginson & Sawir have noted (see also Shamir, 2005). The idea of network refers to electricity, but it can also evoke an early and in many ways still dominant means of global trade, the shipping network that links seaports around the globe, the ports themselves nodes connected by the ongoing ply between them and united too, in a hybridized culture that absorbs and is altered by the influx of outside influences.

Of specific interest for present purposes is the way in which the phenomena of globalization are viewed in terms of the impact and reaction within higher education. Education theorists note that there is a widespread tendency to read globalization in higher education deductively from more general theories of globalization (Marginson & Sawir, 2005, p. 282). But do the ideas and images of network and flows apply to the arena of higher education worldwide? If we look globally at higher education, do we find a "preeminence of social morphology over social action . . . an open structure expanding with shared communication codes highly susceptible to innovation . . . in which the power of flows takes precedence over the flows of power?" (Castells, 2009, p. 501).

A quick glance at any metric seems to suggest not. By almost any measure, the US system overwhelmingly dominates the planet, making the idea of network with a connection of more or less equal nodes seem erroneous. Currently, the US is widely accepted to be the best higher education system globally in both elite and mass sectors (Langan, 2004, p. 17; Altbach et al., 2001). Moreover, it is the largest higher education system, educating over 20 percent of the world's students. America also commands the largest portion of the world's research and development expenditure. Further, the US receives by far the largest number of international students in the world, 28 percent of the total (Bain & Cummings, 2005) and with thousands of institutions, can expand that incoming number almost indefinitely. The mobility of scholars and students worldwide is a major component of the global university network, helping to circulate ideas and also maintaining the power of the major "host" countries in their ideological and research hegemony (Altbach, 1998). To take an example of particular interest to this study, America trains more 4-year engineering graduates per capita than any other country (Zakaria, 2008). While some regions, such as the European Union, or nations, such as Australia, have increased the numbers of incoming students dramatically, overall, the US still commands the highest percentages. Currently, the US attracts more foreign students than the three largest competitors (UK, Germany and France) combined (Altbach, 2004a). The large number of students coming into the US creates a notable contrast to those American students that do go abroad for higher education. Only a small percentage of US students leave the country, and of those that do, most are undergraduates. Almost none get a degree abroad.

Philip Altbach credits the Western university institutionalization of the study of science and its later production as a key factor (1998). Moreover, US universities have been and remain at the center of a knowledge network that includes research institutions, the means of knowledge dissemination such as journals and scientific publishers, as well as a network of scientists. For example, the bulk of the world's scientific literature now appears in English. Scholars in industrialized European countries such as Sweden or the Netherlands often find it necessary to communicate their research findings in English. Even the large Dutch multinational publishers, Elsevier and Kluwer, publish virtually all of their scholarly and scientific books and journals in English (Altbach, 1998).

In addition, thirty-eight of the top fifty universities in the world are in the US (Zakaria, 2008). What is more, the US dominates in international league tables, citation indexes and other metrics of higher education policy and activity from around the world. In fact, the US model has generally come to be accepted as the exemplar of "world class" (for a discussion of "world class" see Deem, Mok & Lucas, 2008; Altbach, 2004a).

Indeed, US dominance in higher education is so immense that the boundaries of that dominion are hard to discern. For example, efforts to similarly be categorized as "world class" spur institutions and nations around the world to model their institutions, higher education policy, and activity around US models.

To cite one vivid example, Frank and Gabler compare Jordan and the US around the year 2000 (2006). Jordan had a gross domestic product per capita one-tenth that of the US. Jordan was a constitutional monarchy of about four million people while the US was a democracy of about 280 million. Jordan was mainly Sunni Muslim, and the US was mainly Protestant Christian. Contrary to what functionalist imagery might predict, the academic emphases at the University of Jordan looked remarkably similar to those found at any US state university of the same period: Faculties of Arts, Business Administration, Science, Medicine, Agriculture, Engineering and Technology, to name a few. Only Jordan's Faculty of Islamic Studies seems distinctive, yet its American analogues are present in departments of theology, or biblical studies. Frank and Gabler show that around the globe from country to country, differences in university priorities are very small and thus do not seem to follow functionalist arguments (2006). With the dominant needs and interests so variable by country, one would expect much greater variation than is currently found if universities were fashioned to respond to functionalist demands. While one cannot say decisively that such isomorphism is direct imitation of the US model, the fact of US domination in so many metrics makes that suggestion far more plausible.

Further analyses of US higher education dominance are centered on the impact or result of its power. Bourdieu and Wacquant, for example, lament the imperialism embedded in the use of "globalization" to make transnational relationships of power appear as a neutral necessity (1999, p. 42). Faulting "symbolic dominion and influence exercised by the USA over every kind of scholarly . . . production through the power of consecration they possess and the material and symbolic profits that researchers in the dominated countries reap from . . . an assumed or ashamed adherence to the model derived from the USA," they attribute to American university research the global stature and power of attraction comparable with those of American cinema, music, software and sports (1999, p. 46). Moreover, they attribute the internationalization of academic publishing key among the factors that have contributed to the domination of "US thought" (1999, p. 46).

How then, can we apply the ideas of a global network to higher education? In short, what are we to make of the power of flows amidst all this power?

Purpose of the Research

To study the flow of the global network of higher education, this book will focus the examination on a particular case study. The objective of this research is to examine an innovation in program planning and development within higher education, specifically, an international multi-institutional graduate degree program in engineering education. However, this study does not presume to attempt to identify the one single truthful account of the planning process of the multi-institutional degree, but rather to explore the complexities of the context.

As Deem (2001) and others have made clear (Marginson & Sawir, 2005), to understand the global flow in higher education we must situate globalization in terms of local individuals and contexts. According to Rizvi and Lingard,

> globalization cannot be viewed as a generalized phenomenon, but rather needs to be seen as a dynamic phenomenon expressed in particular histories and political configurations. Thus, while there are today global policy pressures . . . and discourses, they are manifest in vernacular ways, reflecting the varying cultures, histories and politics within different nations. (preface, 2010)

To observe the manifestations of the global network of higher education, I locate the case study within it, focusing on the collaboration between two nodes of the network. As noted above, US higher education seems to dominate the globe in terms of higher education. In order to examine the flows of the global network of higher education, then, a US institution is an obvious potential site. A second relevant site is Singapore, with its growing global economic importance and stated goal of establishing itself as a global education hub. Therefore, this case study is centered on program planning between a US and a Singaporean institution.

According to Philip Altbach, the research university is the central institution of the 21st century, at the nexus of science, scholarship and the knowledge economies (2007, p. 1). Moreover, it is an international institution that aims for a global reach both in mission and in renown (Altbach, 2007). As the apex of national higher education systems, research universities serve as the model that other types of institutions emulate, which makes their influence greater than their numbers would suggest (Mohrman, Ma & Baker, 2008, p. 5). Furthermore, the transnational network in which they function serves as a conduit for other types of institutions. Therefore this study will examine the phenomenon of the global network of higher education within the context of two specific nodes of that network in the collaboration of two research institutions.

Moreover, research universities serve a key role in the globalization of science. In knowledge based economies, the research university is increasingly linked to national goals of modernization, economic development, and technological advance (Mohrman, Ma & Baker, 2008). In concert with this trend is the growth in what has been called "global science" (Peters, 2006). Distinct from the classical tradition of the international exchange of theories, concepts, and discoveries, global science describes the emerging geography of scientific knowledge and collaboration (Peters, 2006, p. 226). While global science contains vestiges of the university-industry-government research triangle, international factors are colliding with and thus, potentially reconfiguring, the previously dominant structure of the "golden triangle" (Feldman, 1989; Leslie, 1993; Etzkowitz & Leydesdorff, 1997; Peters, 2006). Intensified international competition for knowledge assets, growing recognition of common global problems such as environmental destruction and disease, combined with enormous costs of research development have all contributed to increasing international collaboration in the sciences, what Peters has called the "emerging age of global science" (Peters, 2006, p. 226). Historically at the center of the debate surrounding the "golden triangle," engineering education will be impacted by changes in the structure of research and the funding that sponsors it (Etzkowitz & Leydesdorff, 1997). In many ways then, the development of an international partnership between research institutions in engineering education is a prime location to observe the global network in higher education and the emerging factors that may be directing its flows.

Positioned within the broader historical, economic and cultural context, this localized case study will reappraise the efficacy of global economic and cultural forces as they influence higher education program development. Through the broad lens of economic and cultural globalization and the narrow scope of qualitative case study research, this study investigates "the extent to which societies [localized in this case study to specific higher education institutions] will be able to pick and choose the ways in which, and the degree to which they can participate in a global world" (Burbules & Torres, 2000, p. 17).

Research Questions

To investigate this phenomenon, we will travel to that vital port of Singapore and observe the "export" of US education firsthand. The sites for this case study are a large, Midwestern research university and its partner research institution in Singapore.[1] Taking as the focus a new form of program abroad for US higher education, a multi-institutional PhD program, this case study will explore the uncharted waters in international programs and the borders of this new area.

On one side of the partnership is an example of US engineering higher education, often criticized for being corrupted by its position in what has been called the triple helix of university-industry-government relations (Etzkowitz & Leydesdorff, 1997). As state funding has decreased, US public research institutions have had to widen the scope of their traditional localized focus and nationally based influence and instead follow the emerging trends in global science (Altbach, 2007; see Peters, 2006; Mohrman et al., 2008). Whether this allows for a resurgence of intellectual curiosity within the sciences and an uncorrupted pursuit of knowledge in the higher education science disciplines, or rather, leads to another source of domination by multinational corporations (MNCs) or other national interests remains uncertain. At issue in this case is the extent to which the US model of the "golden triangle" of military agencies, high technology industry, and research universities has become more complex, with the triangle replaced by a complex web of "multi-locational global networks" (Castells, 2009, p. 129).

On the other side of the partnership is the aspiring global knowledge hub of Singapore. Openly striving to be "the Boston of the East," Singapore's pursuit of a US-modeled education hub in the context of the worldwide dominance of the US models seems to represent what Sidhu has called "an open acknowledgment by the government of the reciprocal relationships between power and knowledge" (2006, p. 257). The national drive for the US-style instrumental and entrepreneurial focus in higher education suggests the consolidation of America's dominance, if not as the geopolitical and economic power eclipsing the former colonial master of Britain (Sidhu, 2006), then at least as the globally dominant model of higher education.

Such open inequalities between the two partner institutions make a collaboration seem somewhat unlikely. Given the vastly different historical contexts, educational traditions, and cultural milieu between the two partner institutions, their merger in a degree program raises a number of questions.

First, we must consider the nature of the collaboration between the Midwestern university and the Singaporean university. For example, does this collaboration confirm neoliberal or center to periphery narratives with the US institution acting as hegemon? Where does the power originate, and in which direction does it flow? Moreover, if we view the partnership through the lens of network theories, we must also consider how the codes of communication necessary for this connectivity between institutions are negotiated. Examining the nature of the partnership and the communication that facilitates it can provide an exemplar of the flow of power along the global network connections.

Given the cultural and historical ecologies, we must question what rationales propel faculty and administrators from such different institutions in such different circumstances to pursue this program. Are the rationales economic as much of the literature would have us predict, or are specific research goals serving as rationales for the institutions? To what extent are conceptions of the global higher education network recruited as rationales for the program?

Next, to understand the flow of the global network, we must also consider what barriers emerge in the planning process of this international multi-institutional degree.

For example, in the cosmopolitan milieu of higher education, do cultural differences manifest as barriers to collaboration? Further, do the differing hierarchical positions of the institutions become a constraint to collaboration? And to what extent do internal campus bureaucratic practices and policies hamper this international partnership?

Finally, we consider what potentialities are created through this innovation. What are the potentials for this new model with regard to global trends within the global network in higher education? What potentialities exist for institutions to reconfigure their position within the global network of higher education? Does this partnership signal a disruption of the nationally based university triple helix of university-government-industry funded and directed research, or does this partnership simply reconfigure that structure in a new location?

Significance of the Research

This study illuminates but a few facets of the complexity of economic and cultural globalization, revealing that the effects of globalization on higher education "unfold locally in uneven and centrally unpredictable ways" (Luke & Luke, 2000). Though much has been written about the globalization of higher education, by empirically examining the nature of the connection between two partner institutions, this book aims to add a distinctive analysis to the literature on global networks of higher education. This case provides a unique perspective by capturing the connectivity of this network as it develops between these two very different higher education institutions functioning within different national systems.

At first glance, what we discover appears as another quagmire, as global imaginary and local needs become marooned in inveterate procedures, run aground without the ballast of traditional university roles. A closer examination reveals that and more, as we find narratives of globalization recruited to serve local goals. Further, the shifting hierarchical tides within the global network of higher education causes ripple effects that extend into the network of global science. The negotiation of shared codes of communication results in a hybridized imitation and, some suggest, an exceedingly cautious innovation. Contrary to what neoliberal or center to periphery narratives of globalization might lead us to expect, strong national and local governments, culture, and social relationships all play determining roles in the negotiations and resulting form of collaboration between these higher education institutions.

Plan for the Book

In chapter two, we explore the theoretical positions that underpin the analysis of the study. Beginning from the assumption of the prevalence and reach of what Castells has called the network society, this study focuses on one particular realm of that network society, the global network of higher education. Flowing through this examination of nodes within the global higher education network are questions regarding power and agency. For example, the nation states' power to enact or react to education policy, or to pursue national goals within international law, such as intellectual property law, will be undercurrents in the analysis. Therefore, theoretical interpretations of the flow of power and agency in the global network of higher education are examined in this chapter.

Chapter three first establishes the context and relevance of the case study of an international multi-institutional degree in chemical engineering between a Midwestern university and a Singaporean university. The chapter begins with a review of the terms globalization and internationalization clarifying definitions, then traces the historical development of global trends in international programming in higher education from the colonial period through the period influenced by the market. Following is a discussion of emerging models within what is now recognized as the global network of higher education.

Within this broader context, chapter three examines the national ecology for higher education at both sites of this study. On one side of the partnership is an example of US engineering higher education, often criticized for being corrupted by its position in what has been called the triple helix of university-industry-government relations (Etzkowitz & Leydesdorff, 1997). As state funding has decreased, US public research institutions have had to widen the scope of their traditional localized focus and nationally based influence and instead follow the emerging trends in global science (Altbach, 2007; Peters, 2006; Mohrman et al., 2008). This chapter includes a discussion of how US international programming in higher education has responded to pressures to enter the education marketplace, as well as other contributing factors that underpin the rationales for international engagement in US higher education. Next, this chapter outlines the development of US higher education in the sciences, particularly engineering, revealing criticisms and debates regarding the role of engineering education in the university-industry-government triple helix.

The corresponding section on Singapore details the development of educational policy related to international programs such as the "Global Schoolhouse" policy and the Singapore governments' goals of attracting foreign university expertise through the WCU policy. Included in this section are other related policy developments including that of English language as the working language of Singapore and the development of Intellectual Property policy (IP). In each of these policy directives, this book traces the Singaporean government's reliance on imitation, or various forms of appropriation of models from the West, as an economic development strategy.

Chapter four outlines the methodological assumptions and procedures of the study. Since this research is qualitative with data analyzed inductively, emerging as disparate pieces of evidence are collected and reviewed. In particular, this chapter explains the two main methods employed to understand the case study. First, interviews of participants are used to understand the complexities through perceptions of participants. Second, document analysis validates and triangulates the information gathered in interviews.

The purpose of chapter five is to provide the initial perspectives and the original formulation of objectives of the program planners as they began and then progressed through the initial stages in the development of the international multi-institutional degree. The narrative provides an overview of participants' perceptions of the historical economic and cultural issues that surrounded the original alliance. First, on both sides of the partnership, local economic changes occurred that encouraged participants to pursue partnerships abroad. Moreover, shifting perceptions of globalization and growing recognition of the importance of membership in the global network in higher education leads administrators and faculty on both sides of the original partnership to form this international alliance.

Second, interviews and documents reveal that at the inception of the partnership, participants at both the US and the Singaporean institution were shifting their perceptions regarding their own institution's position as a part of the global network, redefining what role their respective institutions should take with regard to this international engagement. Defying the traditional roles the institutions had previously followed in international programming, both institutions chose to develop a new model to reposition their institutions within the global network of higher education, renegotiating the hierarchical positioning within international engagements.

In the narrative of interviews and document excerpts in chapter six we explore a number of potential barriers encountered by the program planners. Administrative issues ranging from committee approval processes, differences in research and institutional culture, and intellectual property rights threaten the continuation and development of the partnership. Tracing the program's tremulous progress through the approval processes, particularly at the US campus, we can observe one example of how the shared codes of communication essential for global network membership are negotiated.

Because of the US dominance in accreditation and certification bodies, the Singapore institution adopts a number of US academic practices and models in order to meet the requirements of various administrative bodies at the US campus. Furthermore, the Singaporean government and institution intentionally strive to adopt US models in a number of key circumstances. Yet, strategic appropriation of foreign practice is not unique to this case, but instead is in line with policies that the Singapore government and institutions have used since independence. However, it is not only the Singaporean campus that alters policy and procedure through the negotiations. The US campus also capitulates, though gradually, to the partnership model. As we will see, this is not necessarily an adherence to the network model in general, but may also be viewed as a competitive strategy for the institution in order to remain competitive in attracting national and international funding sources, so critical for sustaining high quality programs in the sciences.

Chapter seven provides a thematic review of the findings tracing the rationales, barriers and potentialities of the planning process for the multi-institutional degree as well as discussing the implications for global science and higher education networks suggested by the final approved version of the degree. Finally, this chapter suggests directions for further research and offers some concluding thoughts.

Notes

1. The institutions are referred to as "Midwestern university" and "Singapore university" in compliance with institutional review board requests at both universities.

CHAPTER TWO

Agency and Power within Global Networks

Introduction

This study begins from the assumption of the prevalence and reach of what Castells has called the network society. We focus our attention on one particular realm of that network society, the global network of higher education. The evidence of the increasing connection between higher education institutions around the globe is well documented, but what is less understood is how this network is enacted or manifested on specific nodes of the global higher education network. Moreover, there is a paucity of research examining the increasing connections between global higher education networks and the structural overlap and feedback loops with global science and other global economic and political networks. By empirically examining the nature of connection between two partner institutions, this study aims to add a unique perspective to the literature on global networks and the functions of higher education within them.

Flowing through this examination of nodes within the global higher education network are questions regarding power and agency. For example, the nation states' power to enact or react to education policy, or to pursue national goals within international law, such as intellectual property law, will also be undercurrents in the analysis. Other theoretical interpretations of the flow of power and agency in the global network of higher education will be examined.

In order to observe the collaboration between institutions, we will narrow the scope to their particular localities. The effect of globalizing processes on specific localities is captured by the word 'glocalization,' deriving from the Japanese term dochakuka, loosely translated as "global localization" (Clarke, 2003, p. 191). Using this framework, globalization does not equal worldwide homogenization (Appadurai, 1996). Instead, emphasis on the globalizing process acknowledges a more complex worldview in which change is multidirectional and negotiated differently in specific localities evident in hybridizations, imitations and vernacularizations. Moreover, "glocalization" encourages the understanding of such differences in the context of overarching processes, such as the effects of connectivity and integration. This lens offers the potential for incorporating diverse local experience into the narrative of the network society. As Robertson has noted, "from this perspective the problem becomes that of spelling out the ways in which homogenizing and heterogenising tendencies are mutually implicative" (1990, p. 27).

Recognizing that this analysis occurs from the "inside out," examining from the traditional position of center gazing out to the periphery (Luke & Luke, 2000, p. 286), this study starts with the assumption that there is no objective position from which to observe. This focus allows a perspective that can resist over-generalization, essentilization, and "the export of US scholarly categories" (Bourdieu & Wacquant, 1999, p. 51). Rather than a positivist reading of the events as "evidence" of the universal effects of globalization, this study is primarily interested in the particular, the local adaptations, hybridizations, and vencularizations that occur in this specific program development. It is within these particularities that we will uncover the rationales, possibilities, and barriers that emerge in this planning process of an international multi-institutional degree.

Globalization as Connectivity

Recognizing that globalization is a contested term denoting multifarious debates and discussions including political, economic, and cultural to name just a few, in this study, globalization is taken to signify a source of connectivity, promoting "the intensification of worldwide social [and economic] relations which link distant localities in such a way that local happenings are shaped by events occurring miles away and vice-versa" (Giddens, 1990, p. 64). Burbules and Torres describe globalization "as the increasingly interdependent relationships between economies, nation-states, cultures, and even institutions" (Burbules & Torres, 2000, p. 22). Approaches to connectivity emphasize the role of networks linked by fast air transport and instant electronic communication.

Indeed, some have called networks the dominant metaphor for our times (Scholte & Robertson, 2007, p. 868). Before the 1990s, the concept of "world system" was ubiquitous, but the prevailing metaphors of global analysis have now shifted from such deterministic metaphors of "system" to the multi-centered, informal and flexible notion of flows, webs and networks. Rather than a unitary sense of global order, networks flow in all directions and are not oriented or organized around a controlling source. Therefore, they can function in complex, uncertain global environments.

Powell (1990) and others (see Scholte & Robertson, 2007, p. 867) have described networks as a form of social organization. In contrast to other forms of social organization such as markets or hierarchies, the fluid reciprocity of networks corresponds to the complex and diverse global environment. For example, networks can retain the flexibility of markets but provide higher levels of mutual trust and cooperation than markets, potentially enabling more effective repeated exchanges to take place over time. Networks also retain some of the coordinating functions of hierarchies, but provide a richer framework of shared knowledge than is evident in a more top-down system of organization. Instead, transactions occur through individuals or entities engaged in reciprocal exchange over a period of time (Scholte & Roberston, 2007, p. 870). Each transaction enhances the connectivity that is the distinctive attribute of the network.

Castells' theory of the network society.

To better understand the morphology of this connectivity, we turn to Castells, who has written at length about the structure of this connectivity and flow. This type of interdependence has been described by Castells (2002) as a new social structure.

> The interaction between the revolution in information technology, the process of globalization, and the emergence of networking as the predominant social form of organization constitutes a new social structure: the network society. (p. 548)

Within this global network society, business, government and policy-making, technology, and cultural life are all increasingly organized in a network structure. Castells states that within this network, "society is constructed around flows, the expression of processes dominating our economic, political and symbolic life" (2009, p. 442). These flows are amplified by three elements: (1) technology; (2) the principal geographic nodes and hubs, such as global cities, financial centers or universities; and (3) the dominant, highly mobile, social groups. New communications and information technology such as the Internet allow communication to take place regardless of geographic borders between a multiplicity of interconnected users. At the same time, interpersonal networks among individuals and groups have developed not simply in local face-to-face settings, but also in longer-distance transnational settings. These global networks exist in trade and business, within political elites and international organizations, among scientists and knowledge-based professional groups, among nongovernmental organizations and within migrant and diaspora groups spread across the world.

In Castells' conception, the network society is comprised of a set of interconnected nodes, with the same distance between nodes regardless of actual geographical location. Nodes are the points in the network at which a curve intersects itself. This network is an open structure, able to expand without limits, integrating new nodes indefinitely as long as they are able to share the same codes of communication. Moreover, within the network, space and time are compressed to zero as information and capital are able to travel at the speed of light. As the network expands, the value of belonging to the network increases, along with the penalty for being outside the network (2009). Networks are described by Castells as being subject to unpredictable patterns of development arising from the creative power of such interaction (2009).

Thompson takes issue with Castells' construction of the network society, finding networks to be "just one of a number of governance and coordinative mechanisms" in the international arena (2003, p. 224). Further, he describes the "shadow of hierarchy" and the "shadow of market" that is cast over network organization, particularly international networks. However, by examining a specific example from Castells, we can see that the theory of network society does not negate all remaining power of the nation state or other governance mechanisms, even if he relegates that power in the context of supranational networks. Moreover, hierarchy and market are indeed part of the conception of the network society, though they are demoted from serving as the dominate social form.

Castells' discussion of the network of science and technology.

To use an example particularly relevant to this study, Castells discusses the "selective globalization of science and technology" (2009, p. 124). He explains that basic research, the ultimate source of knowledge, is located primarily in research universities and the public research system around the globe. This academic research system is global, depending on continuous communication in the form of publications, conferences, journals, seminars, academic associations as well as Internet communication. Though the US and Western Europe dominate access to publications, research funds and prestigious appointments, overall, Castells identifies a network of science, albeit in a hierarchically arranged form. Despite being global in scope, Castells acknowledges that the practice of science is skewed toward issues defined by advanced countries with a fundamental asymmetry in the issues taken up by research. To illustrate, problems which are critical for developing countries but do not meet the needs of the market in dominant countries are neglected, for example, cures for malaria or treatment of HIV (Castells, 2009, p. 126).

Science, technology and the business sector, as well as national and international policies, are essential connections for global technological development. Once the technological connection is assured, the process of technology generation and diffusion is organized around transnational production networks. Castells claims that such networks are largely independent of government policy, yet are dependent on national governments to provide the necessary human resources in the form of education and in infrastructure (2009, p. 127).

Castells' portrayal of agency within the network society.

Some have criticized Castells for failing to fully explicate the role of agency within global flows and networks (Sidhu, 2006; Marginson & Sawir, 2005; Thompson, 2003). Indeed, if we look only to Castells' conception of network membership, agency seems to be limited. A hub may be able to "choose" not to join, but then is subject to the consequences of exclusion whatever that might entail for that particular network. In some examples, resisting network membership seems even less of a choice, in the science and technology network discussed previously, for instance. As Castells recognizes, advanced countries control the priorities and thus the direction of development in the global network of science and technology. Less advanced nations may not have the opportunity to even become part of the network due to inefficiencies in technology, infrastructure, or government policy regarding education, for example. Therefore, membership in networks does not clearly denote agency.

Yet beyond network membership, there is also the matter of the shared communication codes. As mentioned, the network depends on shared communication codes in order to function, yet it is unclear to what extent the codes are negotiated or hegemonically imposed on members by more powerful hubs. In his discussion of the global network of science, for example, Castells explains that the network is asymmetrical, but it is still a network, which suggests that the flow of power is, to some extent, moving in all directions.

Though agency is not always fully explicated in Castells' work, he does credit the network as being unpredictable in development, allowing for creativity spurred by interaction to propel the network direction. This unpredictability further suggests some agency at all levels of the network since a structure controlled by strict hegemony would follow predictable patterns of development. Overall, it seems that to clearly map agency and power within the network, specific examples must be examined in order to trace the flow of power through the global flows. To better understand the possibilities of agency within the flow of globalization, we can turn to Appadurai, who locates agency throughout the various "scapes" of globalization.

Appadurai and the flow of globalization.

Arjun Appadurai has also delineated the constitution of connectivity and the flow of globalization. Similar in many respects to the illustration of network, Appadurai develops the image of "scapes," that is, five dimensions of global flows (Appadurai, 1996, p. 33). Ethonoscapes refers to people in motion as workers, tourists, students, refugees and others. Technoscapes refers to rapidly changing technologies moving at high speeds across borders. Financescapes refers to the movement of capital. Mediascapes refers to the electronic capabilities to produce and disseminate information, and Ideoscapes refers to movement of images, particularly the political. These different scapes follow their own logic, overlapping and intersecting each other. They are irregular and fluid (1996). For Appadurai, globalization is not a single homogenizing process, but multiple processes in different sectors or domains of practice.

Agency within Appadurai's description of global flows.

Within these multiple processes, diversification is enhanced as people, ideas, and images all move through non-isomorphistic paths. According to Appadurai, Americanization, or any form of homogenization, is weakened, and even the nation state cannot hold the reigns amidst this free flow of "people, machinery, money, images and ideas" (1996, p. 37). While some have suggested that this view of a weakened state is overstated, particularly evident in the events occurring since September 11, 2001 (Rizvi & Lingard, 2010; Thompson, 2003; Weiss, 1998), clearly Appadurai has allowed for a level of complexity that images of globalization as the "brakeless train wreaking havoc" seem to miss.

Agency and Power within Global Networks

Within the construct of networks and flows exists a continuum of conceptions regarding agency. On one end of the spectrum is the idea of globalization as an irrepressible force, a runaway world (Giddens, 2003). A more tempered view suggests that agency allows actors to resist global influences, while recognizing that some states or entities have more power than others (Jayasuriya, 2001). Finally, we have the view that nation states are losing all power amidst the global flows (Appadurai, 1996). Questions of agency are integral to this study. This case examines the nature of the collaboration between two international partners from opposite sides of the globe, each with distinct histories and traditions, and each with seemingly disparate positions of power. To understand the connection between these two nodes of the global network of higher education, we will need to take into account conceptions of the nation state as well as higher education within global networks.

Nation state within global networks.

In many prominent examples, debates around globalization have centered on the loss of power of the nation state. Burbules and Torres (2000), for example, describe the emergence of supranational institutions whose decisions shape and constrain the policy options for any particular nation state. Others argue that globalization means the overwhelming impact of global economic processes, including processes of production, consumption, trade, capital flow, and monetary interdependence (Jones, 1996; Obstfeld & Taylor, 2003). For still others, globalization denotes the rise of neoliberalism as a hegemonic policy discourse (Burbules & Torres, 2000, pp. 1-2). Noam Chomsky laments that such developments have resulted in "significant decision making shifts . . . into the hands of unaccountable private tyrannies, mostly foreign-based. Meanwhile the public arena is to shrink still further as the state is minimized in accordance with the neoliberal political and economic principles that have emerged triumphant" (1999, p. 95).

These debates about the remaining efficacy of the nation state are, in some respects, beyond the scope of this book, yet issues of state sovereignty will emerge within our study situated in the global network of higher education. Education remains primarily a state function, designed to instill conformity with standards of citizenship and identification with a national tradition. In the US, this nationalized public school system is enacted in a local context, and thus already susceptible to tensions between local and national control. These tensions may become more evident or even exacerbated by the introduction of global forces. According to Morrow and Torres, "the processes of globalization . . . have serious consequences for educational practices and public policies that are highly national in character" (2000, p. 34).

Moreover, issues surrounding the efficacy of the nation state surface in regard to intellectual property (IP) issues. As a tenet the Uruguay Round of the GATT, IP has become the purview of the supranational organizations. Therefore, nation states must acquiesce or suffer the threat of loss of benefits under the General System of Preferences (Knight, 2003). Though not all international higher education programming involves trade agreements, issues of IP rights become a key negotiation factor in a research based program such as the partnership that this study investigates. As Appadurai's image of scapes has illustrated, overlap and intersection of various scapes within globalization necessarily occur. The emergence of these issues within our study of higher education demonstrates again the flow and connectivity emblematic of globalization, even within the overlap and connectivity of theoretical issues that emerge.

Higher education within global networks.

As mentioned in the introduction, at first glance it might seem that the worldwide dominance of US models and institutions of higher education within the global network of higher education fits the image of a runaway freight train far more accurately than of an ever expanding network of shared communication codes. However, by examining differing theoretical portrayals of the role of the university in society, we do find evidence for an expanding global network, albeit one informed by the "shadow of hierarchy" and the "shadow of the market" (Thompson, 2003). Other theoretical conceptions cast the university as the future producer of a transformation in cultural models and thus as an important site of interconnectivity in the knowledge society. These theoretical portrayals provide important context to this study centered on this new form of collaboration between higher education institutions.

Hierarchy and higher education.

According to Bourdieu, the university is "an institution which has been socially licensed as entitled to operate an objectification which lays claim to objectivity and universality" (1988, p. xii). The university presents reality in objective and universal terms in which scientific knowledge appears a universalistic paradigm. These basic parameters are deeply institutionalized in the culture and organization of world society.

Bourdieu and Passeron have argued that education reproduces power by processes of imposition which protect the order of a particular group whose interests are reproduced by means of a culturally mediated structure of power (1996). In this view, dominant groups surrender the power of selection to an academic institution which appears as a perfectly neutral authority thereby disguising social stratification in a "symbolic violence" (1996).

Moreover, Bourdieu explains that higher education is concerned with the consolidation of the mechanisms of selection, legitimation and accreditation. While most of Bourdieu's analysis is centered on the internal structure of power relations within the university, in *The State Nobility* he demonstrates how higher education can reflect the inequalities in society through stratification (1996). Bourdieu shows how a hierarchy of institutions draws from the corresponding hierarchy of class in society, passing cultural capital on to specific stratifications within society. Within this model, the university is not a transformative force, but instead is largely an agent of reproduction. All culture producers, including academia, are not some type of free-floating intelligentsia, but instead, are power-producing agents. The university as a producer of knowledge is deeply embedded in the production of cultural capital. The social practices that constitute the university do not amount to some essential idea that transcends power or power relations in society. Since power is symbolically produced and maintained by cultural models, the university occupies a central, critical position.

Evidence for higher education as hegemon.

If we look at the role that universities have played historically, it is clear that Western dominance in higher education does have roots of "symbolic violence." First, academic institutions were imposed by colonizers in many parts of the world, and indigenous institutional forms were destroyed by the colonizers (Altbach, 1998). In India, for example, the British imposed European patterns and no longer recognized existing traditional institutions.

Moreover, some critics find that this symbolic violence and post-colonial pattern of behavior continue in Western higher education partnerships with less powerful countries. For example, in a discussion of academic partnerships in Africa, Wiley and Root lament the "one-way flows of personnel and knowledge," from the West, "rather than using Third World needs as a basis for creating reciprocal exchanges" (2003, p. 3). For example, in post-apartheid South Africa of the mid-1990s, funding for partnerships surged, yet many South African academics observed that visits of US academics to their campuses and proposals of linkages did not seem oriented toward mutual capacitation (Wiley & Root, 2003, p. 4). Most programs brought American students and scholars to the South African campuses without providing reciprocal opportunities for African students. To be fair, most South African universities have policies that prohibit students from transferring credit, so traditional exchanges are not feasible, yet many US institutions stopped short of creating true reciprocity through other nontraditional means. Furthermore, almost none of the US institutions have shared the "profits" from the tuition and fees collected in the US (Wiley & Root, 2003). On the one hand, such partnerships demonstrate the development of the global network of higher education made possible by factors like the mobility of scholars and students and communication technology. Still, on the other hand, we can see that this network is not free of hierarchal or market driven interactions.

Despite these shadows of hierarchy and market forces, facets of the current global network of higher education defy strict post-colonial patterns. For example, a colonial past does not account for the fact that the Western academic models continue to be followed in former colonies. Moreover, countries that were never colonized, such as Japan, China and Thailand, also follow Western models (Altbach, 2007). Even the one remaining fully non-Western institution, the Al-Azhar University in Cairo, is now organized along Western lines (Altbach, 1998).

While we must be ever mindful of the colonial past, not discounting or dismissing any hierarchal shadow that it still casts into the present, we must also not assume a colonial or post-colonial interpretation of relationships and interactions. In the examples mentioned, it is unclear if "symbolic violence" is leading institutions to follow Western/US models or if there are other explanations. Researchers and scholars must be open to the new patterns emerging and the attendant repositioning, reimagining, that may occur within this new social structure. For example, Luke and Luke argue that "globalization is neither a story of rapacious Western multinationals nor hapless Eastern victims. . . rather such forces dovetail in unpredictable and unsystematic ways in to local histories and relations" (2000, p. 286). The new social structure of network society as put forth by Castells and by Appadurai create the possibility for new patterns of social organization, even if under the shadow of hierarchy and markets.

Higher education as mediator of discourses.

Within the changes brought to society through globalizing forces, some theorists portend a changing or developing role for the university in future society (Mohrman, Ma, & Baker, 2008; Altbach, 2007). In sharp contrast to an agent of reproduction of power structures, an alternative conception set forth by Delanty casts the university, or at least the potential future of the university, as a mediator among discourses. According to Delanty, of all the social resources, it is knowledge that lends itself most easily to globalization because of its depersonalized and universalistic nature (2001). Further, because of the massification of higher education, knowledge is diffused throughout society more than ever before. It is no longer confined to the elite class only, but is publicly available. Therefore, professional knowledge and lay knowledge have become indistinguishable. The democratization of knowledge has been accompanied by the growing contestability of knowledge claims. Delanty finds that, "as more and more actors are being drawn into the field of knowledge production the self-legitimation of the older knowledge elites becomes less certain" (2001, p. 5).

Delanty argues that the current situation amounts to a major epistemic or cognitive shift. Changes in the mode of knowledge are related to a transformation in cultural models as well as far reaching changes in the institutional framework of society (2001, p. 5). Delanty extends the definition of knowledge from the application of information (Gibbons, 1995) to include "a cognitive capacity that is related to the production of cultural models and institutional innovation" (2001, p. 5). Delanty argues that the future significance of the university is that it can be the most important site of interconnectivity in the knowledge society. By resisting the inclination to become a self-referential bureaucratic organization, and relinquishing old ideals of enlightening society, Delanty locates the central task of the twenty-first century university to become a key actor in the public sphere capable of mediating among the production of knowledge as a set of discourses cutting across institutional and epistemological forms (2001, p. 17).

Evidence for the possibility of mediator role.

Though Delanty clearly outlines this new role for the university as a potential hub of interconnectivity in the knowledge society, it requires the university to cast off much of its current structure. Therefore, such a conception is difficult to pin down to any empirical form. Yet Delanty is not alone in imagining the future of the university as a hub of interconnectivity. In fact, by looking to the arena of international programming, potential examples of this interconnectivity function begin to emerge.

For example, in a somewhat similar vein, Bernardo explains in a discussion of the Philippine system of higher education, in a globally distributed knowledge production system, different institutions will have different capabilities and resources to bring to an international partnership. Institutions in developing countries like the Philippines are, as previously mentioned, currently at risk of serving merely as conduits to foreign institutions (2003). However, if a mutually cooperative arrangement is formed, with both the institutions serving as equal partners, "resources could be shared to meet complex external demands and higher quality standards" (Bernardo, p. 262). Bernardo cites improvement in curricular programs, strengthened qualifications of faculty members, improved standards in libraries, laboratories, and other learning materials as well as opportunities in research capabilities as potential benefits to Philippine institutions through international partnerships. US institutions could benefit through study abroad programs, increased international enrollment and research opportunities.

This broadly sketched hypothetical example of a US/Philippines partnership captures imagined benefits and an envisioned ideal for educators that may enjoin them to pursue international programming. However, such theoretical concepts do little to illuminate the actual functioning of the global network of higher education or to reveal the nature of its connectivity. In contrast, this case study will undertake specific research on partnerships with an institution from a nation of otherwise inequitable standing with the US in order to better understand the potentialities and barriers of such endeavors.

In these theoretical portrayals of the university role in society, it is clear that the university has served as a conduit of power. What remains unclear is the nature of the flow of power through the global network in higher education. In order to better understand the functioning of the network of higher education, this study closely examines two nodes of that network and the attempt to connect the programs in an international joint degree. Through this close examination, the study attempts to map the flow of power through the flows of globalization.

Local Agency and Globalization

In order to understand the flow of power and agency within the flows of globalization, specific local examples are necessary. As Appadurai and others have noted, global flows always come up against local and national histories, cultures and politics (1996) becoming vernacularized in local cultures (Rizvi & Lingard, 2010).

Pieterse's culture and globalization.

To understand the nature of this international collaboration in higher education, this research is specifically concerned with the way in which local cultures might engage both with each other and with globalizing trends. Of use here are the theories of Jan Nederveen Pieterse, who has outlined three distinct views on the ways in which cultures interact through forces of globalization (2004). As we will see, each of these views portrays a differing concept of agency for the local cultures.

First is the "clash of cultures" view expressed by writers like Samuel Huntington in which cultural factions are viewed to be in perpetual, probably inevitable conflict, even combat with each other. Second is the notion of "McDonaldization" (Ritzer, 2004), which suggests the domination of one culture over others in which the less dominant culture gets erased or adapts to such an extent that it has lost its distinctiveness. In the third view is hybridization, or mélange, or syncretism, in which local cultures borrow, exchange, interpret and blend outside influence into the local.

The differences between these various conceptions can again be recognized as degrees of agency on the part of the interacting cultures. As we saw earlier in our review of theories regarding agency and the nation state or agency and higher education, the distinction between competing theories rests on "the extent to which societies will be able to pick and choose the ways in which, and the degree to which they can participate in a global world" (Burbules & Torres, 2000, p. 17). This book demonstrates that like Jan Nederveen Pieterse's third view, hybridization, mélange, or syncretism result when cultures interact with each other due to forces of globalization. This case study traces the development of these indigenizations as well as the push-pull factors in which they occur.

Robertson's "glocalization."

In addition to Nederveen Pieterse's elucidation of the globalization of cultures, the effect of globalizing processes on specific localities is captured by the word "glocalization," deriving from the Japanese term dochakuka, loosely translated as "global localization" (Clarke, 2003, p. 191). This term allows conceptualization of how global change is negotiated within a local existence. In Japan, the term was originally used by marketing experts to explain that though Japanese products had global application and reach, they would need to be localized, or made palatable and suitable, for local tastes and interests. Now the term itself has been exported and vernacularized to capture the variance that occurs locally through globalization.

Khondker has argued that there is a distinction between processes of glocalization and hybridization. He defines glocalization as the blending and mixing of two or more processes, one of which is local. Hybridization, in contrast, does not rely on a local component. He sites Singaporean higher education as a hybrid version comprised of the British model and the US model. For Khondker, it is not an example of "glocalization" because it is a blend of two foreign systems (2004).

This study argues from a slightly different position. For this study, I will use glocalization to refer to the process by which outside influences, products, or even ideas are locally adapted. The result is the hybridization, vernacularization or indigenization. Referring back to Khondker's example, I find that the Singaporean higher education system is a hybridization occurring through glocalization, containing elements of the British and American systems, combined with elements that are uniquely Singaporean, even in the type and measure of the blend. This study argues that since education practices are always enacted locally, any outside force is therefore likely to be indigenized or hybridized to a greater or lesser extent.

As Appadurai has shown, globalization does not equal homogenization (1996). Instead, emphasis on globalizing process acknowledges a more complex worldview in which cultural change is multidirectional and negotiated differently in individual localities. Moreover, "glocalization" encourages the understanding of such differences in the context of overarching processes, such as the effects of connectivity and economic integration. In this sense, "glocalization" provides a perspective which offers the potential for incorporating local experience and diversity into grand narrative. From this lens, "it is not a question of either homogenization or heterogenization but rather of the ways in which both of these two tendencies have become features of life across much of the . . . world" (Robertson, 1990, p. 27).

Conclusion

Beginning with the assumption of the prevalence and reach of what Castells has called the network society, this chapter broadly outlines this new social form. Moreover, as Appadurai has shown, different scapes follow their own logic, overlapping and intersecting each other. They are irregular and fluid. Globalization is not a single homogenizing process, but multiple processes in different sectors or domains of practice.

This study will be particularly focused on the global network of higher education. Within the global higher education network are questions regarding power and agency. The multidirectional forces that drive the expansion and continued development of the network suggest that neither theories of coercion or new modes of knowledge production dictated by society can fully explain the complexities inherent in such connectivity. In order to examine empirically the collaboration between institutions, I will narrow the scope to their specific localities. The effect of globalizing processes on specific localities is captured by the word "glocalization" (Clarke, 2003, p. 191). This study will consider the ways in which change is multidirectional and negotiated differently in specific localities evident in hybridizations, indigenizations and vernacularizations.

CHAPTER THREE

Local Context in Global Flows

Introduction

To situate this research, we trace the historical development of global trends in international programming in higher education from the colonial period through the period influenced by the market. Following is a discussion of emerging models within what is now recognized as the global network of higher education.

Because our study will be positioned within a local context, we survey the historical, political, and cultural context of each site. This chapter examines the national ecology for higher education in both of the sites of this study, the US and Singapore. First, this chapter traces the historical development of US higher education with a thematic emphasis on its international heritage and subsequent development of localism. These conflicting tendencies inform the milieu from which US institutions pursue international engagement. Following is a discussion of how US international programming in higher education has responded to pressures to enter the education marketplace, as well as other contributing factors that underpin the rationales for international engagement in US higher education. Next, this chapter outlines the development of US higher education in the sciences, particularly engineering, revealing criticisms and debates specific to this discipline in which this case study is situated.

The corresponding section on Singapore details the development of educational policy related to international programs such as the "Global Schoolhouse" policy and the Singapore government's goals of attracting foreign university expertise through the WCU policy. Included in this section are other related policy developments including that of English as the working language of Singapore and the development of Intellectual Property policy (IP). In each of these policy directives, this study traces the Singaporean government's reliance on imitation, or various forms of appropriation of models from the West, as an economic development strategy.

In sum, this chapter establishes the relevance and context of this case study of an international multi-institutional degree in chemical engineering between a Midwestern university and a Singaporean university.

Conceptions of Internationalization and Globalization in Higher Education

Much has been written about the impact of globalization on higher education, yet the terms used to describe both the effects and the causes are sometimes confounded. Efforts at internationalization are often conflated with globalization, with international education portrayed both as the cause and effect of global forces (Altbach, 2004b; Qiang, 2003). Green and Olson argue that globalization and internationalization are linked but not synonymous concepts (2003, p. 3). Others see globalization and internationalization as distinct, with globalization a primarily economic phenomenon and internationalization a phenomenon linked to more traditional concepts of national culture, politics, and history. For example, Reichert and Wachter (2000) explain that globalization refers to forceful changes in the economic, social, political, and cultural environment brought about by global competition, the integration of markets, increasingly dense communication networks, information flows, and mobility. For many theorists, globalization is a relatively uncontrolled process, determined mainly by fierce economic competition on a global scale, and by rapid advances in information and communication technology (Qiang, 2003).

Internationalization, in contrast, is based on conscious action (Knight, 2001). To illustrate, internationalization of the university is frequently portrayed as a response to the challenges brought about by globalization (Green & Olson, 2003). Within this framework, then globalization is a conglomeration of forces impacting higher education, while internationalization is a planned, controlled action, often taken in response to globalization. Bauman finds that globalization refers primarily to global effects notoriously unintended and unanticipated, rather than global undertakings, which might include international education (Bauman, 1998). Internationalization necessarily occurs within this "no man's land" (Bauman, 1998) of the global era.

Globalization, then, has resulted in a greater impetus for internationalization. Since new technology, ease of travel, economic integration and environmental interdependence diminish some types of barriers among nation-states, the imperative to know other societies and cultures increases (Green & Olson, 2003, p. 3). Globalization becomes the justification, a part of what Rizvi has termed the social imaginary (2004), that demands students be prepared to function in a globally linked world.

If we take the US use of this terminology as an example, a shifting emphasis within higher education's international programming and resulting use of terminology becomes apparent. Until the later part of the twentieth century, US universities' primary exchanges with the outside world were couched in terms of "international education." The term itself indicates that such programs are distinct from the rest of education and exist as a separate undertaking. In practice, the result of this parallel concept was that international learning experiences were not incorporated into a university's main curriculum in a prominent way. Typically they were marginalized and poorly integrated into the institution's mission, strategic plan, structure, and funding priorities (Green & Olson, 2003). Examples were international teaching and programs that constitute separate domains such as area studies, foreign languages, or specific sections within disciplines, such as world history or world literature. Study abroad for students, frequently serving a minority of students, was primarily limited to majors from these departments and disciplines. Likewise, research abroad was primarily limited to faculty from these same domains (Green & Olson, 2003).

Now, educators pursue the traditions of international education within the new globally competitive paradigm of international programs.[1] With the growing acceptance of the concept of globalization has come a renewed emphasis on international programs within institutions in the United States as well as globally (Qiang, 2003). The term internationalization is widely used in other countries and has gained currency in the US. The use of the verb form *to internationalize* suggests a move from description to action, a process rather than a description of a specific set of activities (Green & Olson, 2003). Jane Knight defines internationalization as the process of integrating international and intercultural dimensions into all the functions of the university, including teaching, research, and service functions of the institution (2003).

Globalization is recruited as a rationale for internationalizing higher education campuses through international education programs. Widening the scope outward from the US, historical patterns in forms of international education programs are evident on a global scale.

Global Patterns of Development of International Programs

To situate this study within the broad frame of global trends, the following outline traces the changing interpretations and functions of international programming in higher education globally. While recognizing that the categories do overlap and do not follow a precise timeline, delineating the forms of programs abroad of universities reveals global patterns in the shifting rationales for internationalization.

Colonial model.

Before WWII, student mobility was mostly linked to various colonial arrangements designed to develop a local elite that was sympathetic to the economic and political interests of the colonial powers (Rizvi, 2009). Primarily for undergraduates, international education was largely one directional and asymmetrical. Numbers of students engaged in international education were low. International education served mainly as a type of finishing school, justified in terms of "the civilizing mission of education" (Rizvi, 2009). During this period, both the US and Singapore, the sites of our study, were recipients of this mission. For the US, international education primarily meant study abroad for elite students to attend German institutions (Thelin, 2004), or less frequently, British institutions. For Singapore, Britain served as a type of finishing school for a few elite students. Until the Chinese community forced the establishment of the first higher education institutions, Singapore had no higher education system of its own (Lim, 1995, p. 70).

Development model.

International education served an important function during the reconstruction efforts after WWII, offering training for foreign experts and development assistance through technology and expertise (Thelin, 2004). In the US and many other Western countries, international higher education developed in the post-World War II era as a form of foreign aid (Kerr, 1991). In fact, historically, the most common type of overseas operation for US institutions is development assistance programs. Since World War II, American higher education institutions have pursued international programs abroad with developmental goals. The US government has historically relied on higher education to build bridges to foreign institutions and intellectual elites, many of whom were alumni of US institutions (Wiley & Root, 2003).

Bringing students from other countries to importing institutions was intended to provide those students the opportunity to gain valuable skills that could help them rebuild or develop their own nations upon their return home. Moreover, this cross-cultural interaction and the resulting exchange of ideas were designed to spur international understanding for students on the home campus and create bonds of cultural understanding. Well-known programs in the US such as Fulbright and the Peace Corps were supplemented by thousands of smaller programs with similar practices (Thelin, 2004). The frequently stated goal of such programs was nothing less than world peace.

During the Cold War, the US information agency was active in academic exchanges, broadening the Fulbright Programs, and by the 1980s, providing seed funding to encourage more partnerships between US and foreign institutions in order to increase US influence around the globe (Wiley & Root, 2003). Beyond providing assistance, cold war policies began to influence the direction of development programs and often operated "in competition" with similarly directed programs of the Soviet Union (Rizvi, 2009).

Despite cold war manipulations, development assistance programs are generally aimed at meeting the needs of the host site or host region. These programs attempt to assist the local population through the export of expertise. Such programs tend to follow the exporting nation's models of operation. In fact, in some cases, the ethos of specific national models of higher education is itself part of the development contribution. Recipients expect to learn imported expertise according to foreign methods.

Such programs continue. Operated by anyone from individual faculty, departments, universities, or through consortia, these projects serve to build local institutions abroad, improve infrastructure, provide local training, and other forms of development assistance directly to governments or through civil society organizations. In the US, for example, grants funded through the United States Agency for International Development (USAID) and corporate partnerships fund many of these projects.

The market driven model.

By the early 1980s, international programming became increasingly determined by market factors, often driven by neo-liberal assumptions (Rizvi, 2009). Scholars locate a number of underlying forces converging to create this shift in higher education to a market driven model of international programs in higher education: the growing competition among traditional nonprofit universities and colleges; the impact of new providers of higher education, including for-profit degree granting institutions, virtual programs and corporate programs; the impact of digital technology; the dependence of political leaders on market forces to structure higher education; and the globalization of higher education (Newman, Couturier & Scurry, 2004).

Competition increased between traditional, nonprofit institutions, degree-granting for-profit universities, virtual online programs, corporate universities and certificate programs. Moreover, the competition universities face for students became global, with the growing mobility of students and capital. Currently attracting large numbers of international students has become one of the hallmarks of an "internationalized" campus (Green & Olson, 2003). International students are, of course, still appreciated for the cultural diversity they bring to campus, yet the potential economic benefit to institutions and their community is increasingly recognized and valued.

Another example of the market's new prominence in higher education is the increasing use of advertising. According to Newman et al., admissions offices are shifting their purpose from selecting a balanced class to attracting the largest numbers of applicants. Moreover, many universities now hire public relations firms to make sure that they receive their share of favorable mention in the media, an investment in "brand management." Advertising, once seen as inappropriate, or even crass, is now commonplace. Polished websites, email, direct mail and phone recruiting are on the rise (2004, p. 12).

Furthermore, brands are not designed for only a domestic or local market, but are worldwide in reach. The aggressive pursuit of international markets by universities is a phenomenon still being characterized by researchers. Marginson (1995) refers to this as the "marketization" of higher education, and futher, Considine et al. (2001) use the term "enterprise university" to characterize universities whose managers are focused on generating income and international prestige. Slaughter and Leslie (1997) use the term "academic capitalism" because it represents for them the inherent clash of cultures and value systems. Ziman (1994) argues that the structural nature of the change is so profound that we are now in a period of "post-academic science."

Perhaps one of the most vivid examples of the market influence in global higher education is its new position in the global trade agreements. In 2000, the US successfully spearheaded a campaign in the WTO to include education as a "service industry" under the purview of the General Agreement on Trade and Services (GATS) (Knight, 2003). As a service industry, higher education is now a tradable commodity. Nations import education when they allow foreign nations to open a campus, send students abroad for education, and allow distance education from abroad. Nations export education when they establish a foreign campus, operate international distance learning programs, and though counterintuitive, when international students come to campus. The terminology "export" and "import" refers to the movement of the funds, not necessarily the students.

The GATS agreement has the power of international law and is not revocable for any of the WTO's member nations. Education trades internationally in the form of market access. That is, countries can grant access to their education industry, which then allows foreign institutions to set up shop as a branch campus or to import through distance learning programs. Because of the most favored nation principle, countries cannot pick and choose who has access. Individual countries have the power to determine the degree of market access, but if access is granted to one country, then it must be granted to all member nations (Knight, 2003). For example, if a country is allowed to establish a branch campus, then all nations must have that same right. Moreover, access to industries can be traded across sectors. Therefore, a nation could trade access to education within its borders for access to the communication markets, for example, in another country. Access to any "market" (nation) is decided by trade specialists and treaties, rather than local institutions or governments. In fact, in the US, only the President with the input of the US Trade Representative has the power to act in this trade agreement. Further, GATS is not neutral. Its stated purpose is progressive liberalization with increased pressure for further reduction of "trade barriers" or restrictions to national markets with each round of negotiations (Knight, 2003).

In addition to its position as a tradable commodity, higher education increasingly looks to business as a model of increasing "revenues" and expanding "production" (Knight, 2003). In what Knight has called "trade-creep" institutions now speak of strategic plans, branding, and marketability of programs (2003).

Newman et al. find the trend toward competition amplified as politicians use market forces, rather than regulation, as a means to control costs and increase productivity (2004, p. 2). The trend is a movement from broader, system-wide regulation to specific agreements with the individual institutions, frequently including revisions of mission statements and built in measures of accountability. As capital has become mobile through global markets, politicians have used global market forces to increase competition for higher education and compel institutions and their public service to submit to greater accountability following a business model (Slaughter & Leslie, 1997). Newman et al. demonstrate a growing interest in shifting from dependence on regulation and oversight to using the market as a means of ensuring public purposes (2004). Despite initial and even some continued resistance, researchers find that educators are coming to accept the business model for higher education management (Marginson, 1995; Slaughter & Leslie, 1997).

However, some critics fear that this shift toward market forces may in fact cause a growing gap between the purposes associated with the public good that need to be served and the reality of how higher education is functioning (Newman et al., 2004). Newman et al. find that the search for truth is being rivaled or replaced by a search for revenues. They argue that as the gap between higher education's rhetoric of its public purpose and the reality of its current performance grows, continued public support of higher education will be imperiled. Further, they assert that there is not necessarily a "market" for public purposes. Markets may bring benefits, but they may also bring unexpected or undesired effects. Those without resources and without access to information can be at a great disadvantage in a market system (2004). They argue that a controlled market is important for higher education and point to the US GI Bill as an example of the successful use of a controlled market to stimulate and improve higher education (2004, p. 43).

Of course, there may in fact be potential benefits beyond profit for the increased marketization and corresponding competition in higher education. Newman et al. agree that societies can gain from the entry of global higher education institutions into their communities. In cases where the existing institutions "are set in their ways and outmoded in their approach, new institutions are bringing a breath of fresh air, pushing older institutions to new action" (2004, p. 27).

Yet there are also undoubtedly great risks inherent in education aimed primarily at generating funds. Education patterned on speculative business ventures carries the innate risks of the business model. To take a specific example, following the outsourcing of many multinational corporations, higher education has made similar efforts to outsource by opening up campuses, degrees and programs around the world. Many of these programs have failed, with perhaps the most noticeable examples in Japan, where of the more than 20 US campuses operating there in the 1990s, only one remains today. Of relevance to this study is the closure of Australia's University of New South Wales just three months after accepting its first batch of 148 students at the branch campus in Singapore. Similarly, citing differences over control and funding, Britian's Warwick refused an offer to open a campus in Singapore, and Johns Hopkins University closed when it was unable to meet key performance indicators (KPI) as set by Singapore's government (Hoong, 2007).

Of course, outsourcing in business has similarly suffered mixed results. For example, in the 1990s, most of the foreign companies that set up shop in China found that they were wrong about the profit predictions, even though the Chinese incomes more than doubled in that decade (Meredith, 2007, p. 65). Though Chinese policy requires partnerships with local companies in order for foreign companies to operate in China, conflict arose when differing business practices and political ideas clashed. The Chinese and the foreigners were, as the Chinese saying goes, "sleeping in the same bed, dreaming different dreams" (Meredith, 2007, p. 64).

It perhaps should come as no surprise, then, that a number of international education projects have met with mixed rates of success. For traditionally locally oriented higher education institutions, such endeavors are still relatively new and present myriads of challenges, including cultural, political, and economic, that are not yet fully surmountable even by the business community from which they are modeled. But a failed education institution carries consequences different than a failed business enterprise. Students and their families, faculty, administrators and the surrounding community all suffer not only the loss of the traditional benefits of education, including personal enrichment and economic advancement, but now also suffer the loss amplified by globalization rhetoric. With the heightened importance of higher education comes a greater penalty for a disruption or unsuccessful end of a program or institution and the resulting (real or perceived) marginalization for the resulting abandoned students.

Emerging rationales and models in international programming.

Within the global higher education ecology, new models of international programming are being developed spawned from new rationales, in many cases with a stated emphasis on global network membership. These new models often rely on elements of both the development model, which emphasizes social and cultural development, capacity building and international relations, and the market model, which emphasizes global competition, brand management, and revenue creation for institutions. Yet, these new models carry distinctions in both form and function. According to Gürlz, "with the advent of the global knowledge economy, new rationales have emerged, or the classical ones have assumed new dimensions and contents (2008, p. 140; Mohrman, Ma & Baker, 2008). Such new rationales can manifest in new program types or in new incarnations of previous models.

For example, the tradition of capacity building has assumed new forms in the global knowledge economy. Now, technology transfer is a variant of capacity building, and it can take the form of "electronic media, Petri dishes, and more importantly, in human brains (Gürlz, 2008, p. 142). With universities serving as the knowledge factories in the knowledge economy (Slaughter & Leslie, 1997) the import of education through distance learning, online courses, or programs offered abroad is used to spur local development. Moreover, the establishment of research centers and laboratories connected with universities are used to stimulate local industry development through technology transfer (Harding et al., 2007).

Altbach and Balan, and others, locate research institutions at the nexus of science, scholarship and the new knowledge economies, and thus as the central institution of the 21st century (2007). Moreover, internationalization is a key dimension of the research university (Altbach, 2007). Almost all world class universities are in the US or other English speaking countries or a few industrialized nations. Articulating an emergent manifestation of the development model, Altbach argues that all countries need academic institutions linked to the global academic system of science and scholarship so that they can participate in advanced scientific developments (2007). However, "research universities are inevitably more expensive to operate and require more funds than other academic institutions. They are also more selective in student admissions and faculty hiring and stand at the pinnacle of an academic system" (Altbach, 2007, p. 5). Recognizing the enormous costs of creating and sustaining such an institution, Altbach recommends academic alliances between poorer institutions and leading institutions in order to distribute greater technological capacity to participate in global science (2007).

Other variations within the development model are emerging under the rationales influenced by the global knowledge economy. Traditionally, developing nations have expected to repatriate foreign educated citizens as a capacity building strategy. Now, a number of countries with advanced higher education systems are recruiting foreign students and providing incentives for them to join the workforce of the host county. Sending countries are said to benefit from the remittances that expatriates make to their home countries, yet the sending countries do not benefit from the return of their citizen as trained expert as was the norm in times past. Knight has called this "human resource development through brain power" (2007), similar to what Gürlz has called "the developed-nation-version of capacity building" (2008, p. 142).

Another emergent rational and model in the global knowledge economy is "strategic alliances" (Gürlz, 2008). Rather than political or cultural rationales of previous eras, "countries are increasingly viewing the internationalization of postsecondary education as a foreign policy tool to establish strategic alliances bilaterally, regionally, and multilaterally to gain both a political advantage and to increase their competitiveness in global markets" (Gürlz, 2008, p. 142). Moving beyond strict market imperatives, in such alliances, global network connection becomes the primary goal.

Programs designed to create such alliances can take various forms. One example is the network model in which institutions link geographically separate institutions through a functional integration with a relatively intense sharing of resources and a relatively flat hierarchy between the connected campuses. According to Olds, "flows of what might have been viewed as 'proprietary knowledge' occur across space between campuses and between firms based in campus city regions" (2007, p. 971). The network model functions particularly well in global cities; a socio-economic formulation that is built upon global flows of people, ideas and technologies (Olds, 2007, p. 972). Networks of institutions can involve from two to many campuses linked through joint programs, joint degrees, or joint research efforts.

The site of this study is one such emergent model in international programming, a jointly awarded multi-institutional degree between two research institutions, one from the middle of the center, a Midwestern research institution, while the other, the edge of the periphery, in Singapore. Not strictly based on market or development models, yet containing elements of both, this new type of program represents emergent goals of global connection, global competition, and global collaboration. Before examining the specifics of that program form, this study will further survey the national contexts in which this program has been developed.

National Context of the Study

Clark Kerr has argued that there are currently two laws of motion propelling institutions of learning around the world. The first, the further internationalization of learning, has been discussed in the previous section. In the discussion that follows, this narrative considers the second. That is, "the intensification of the interest of independent nation-states in the conscious use of these institutions [of higher education] for their own selected purposes" (1991, p. 17). This section begins with a discussion of the US, its cultural framing and the historical factors that influence its international programming and its engineering education in particular. Next, we take a corresponding view of Singapore and the "selected purposes" it has for higher education.

US Higher Education's Cultural Framing

US higher education's international heritage.

Philip Altbach traces all universities to one European ancestor, the University of Paris, in France in the 13th century (1998, p. 22). The French institution put the professor at the center of the university and enshrined academic freedom as an important part of the ethos. This model spread and adapted in other parts of Europe. Under the leadership of Wilhelm von Humboldt, German higher education was given significant resources by the state and took the responsibility for research aimed at national development and industrialization. The German university also established graduate education and the doctoral degree as a major focus of the institution (Altbach, 1998, p. 22).

By the nineteenth century, universities were important in establishing the cultural foundations of national identity. With the decline of Latin as a common language and the rise of the vernacular, the university was crucial in promoting national languages, national literatures and national geography.

Universities collected and defined ethnographic and cultural material without which national cultural narratives, consciousness and national imaginaries would not have been possible (Altbach, 1998). A national academic elite developed replacing the cosmopolitanism of earlier times. Delanty refers to Oxford and Cambridge as examples where the entire national elite was educated and thus replicated (2001, p. 35). This emphasis on local cultural narratives gets exported and then adapted into the US system of higher education. "To the English concept of the general culture of the educated gentleman and the German concept of scholarly research for its own sake, the American university added another dimension; namely, that higher education to justify its own existence should seek to serve actively the basic needs of American life" (Brubacher & Rudy, 1997, p. 394).

Gürlz credits the study abroad experiences of American students in the late nineteenth and early twentieth centuries in Germany with the subsequent adoption of German research university models in the US. Many of the founders of US research institutions as well as early leaders of those institutions were educated in Germany and, thus, fashioned the developing campuses in the US on the German research model (Brubacher & Rudy, 1997; Gürlz, 2008, p. 132). But it wasn't just returned study abroad students who endeavored to recreate the German model in the US. Administrators like Daniel Coit Gilman toured German universities to recruit staff and learn about their organization before taking up the presidency at Johns Hopkins at the turn of the twentieth century (2008, p. 132).

US higher education's heritage of localism.

In concert with endeavors to emulate the German and British higher education models, American educators took European innovations and further transformed higher education by intensifying the links between the university and society through the concept of service and direct relationships with industry and agriculture (Altbach, 1998, p. 22). The Land-grant model developed in the US and included high-level research, high commitment to the needs of society and industry, and expanded access for students beyond the elite classes. These land-grant institutions epitomized American ideals of access for all citizens, as well as a close connection to the public it served. Within these land-grant institutions, curriculum increasingly represented what Jefferson, Franklin and Eliot had advocated for earlier democratic, public service courses. According to Brubacher and Rudy, "[f]or [educators], and more and more for the American public, the main yardsticks of value for the college and university came to be utility and 'social efficiency'" (1997, p. 118). President James of Illinois envisioned the state's university as "a great civil service academy, preparing the young men and women of the state for the civil service of the state, county, municipality and the township" (quoted in Lucas, 1994, p. 176).

By the late nineteenth century, "localism" – the essential quality of civic pride that developed the "booster college", had developed into what Thelin asserts as the strongest characteristic of the varied institutions of the time (2004, p. 107). In fact, differences resulting from this local orientation were magnified. Today, Harvard, Yale, and Princeton are lumped into a single category of the Ivy League, but in the late 1800s, each institution represented a distinct tradition and commitment (Thelin, 2004). Moreover, most students attended their own local university or college until well into the 20th century (Thelin, 2004).

Impact of localism on internationalization.

American institutions' approach to internationalization retains the cultural emphasis on university service to its local community, particularly for large research institutions, most of which were developed specifically to advance local agriculture, mining and other industry. Local pressures dictate that international programs be seen in concert with this goal. Some institutions suffer public outcry if they appear *too* internationally focused. These tensions can be exacerbated by public perception that local tax money is supporting the local institution, while at the same time, institutions struggle to thrive because of ongoing cuts in that public funding. An example of this tension is found in the Chicago, Illinois, newspapers regarding the University of Illinois at Urbana-Champaign's proposal to increase international student enrollments, which was perceived to be "taking seats from local students" (Goudie, 2006). This criticism is most acute when it is perceived that universities are importing students or exporting technology at the expense of local students or industry. Such pressures continue to affect international program development for US Land-grant research institutions and other public institutions as well.

Rationales for developing an international program abroad.

Despite underlying resistance to an overemphasis on international education, US institutions are pressured from within campus and by outside stakeholders, such as the federal government and potential employers, to develop international programming, particularly in ways that seem to directly benefit the local community and students.

One example is through study abroad programs. Currently, the number of students who study abroad is rising, but many US educators and other stakeholders find that there is much room for growth. For example, students in professional programs such as Engineering and Education lag furthest behind with less than 5% of students going abroad, despite an increasing number of programs aimed at these groups. Overseas programs developed specifically to increase the numbers of US students studying abroad continue to rise. Because the US school calendar does not always mesh with foreign institutional schedules, and because US students commonly lack the language skill for direct enrollment in foreign universities, US institutions are developing new forms of programs in order to facilitate students studying abroad.

Additionally, federal policies affecting everything from biomedical research to international student visas also exert pressure on US universities to seek foreign research sites and direct access to international students and faculty on foreign soil. After the September 11th attacks, changes in immigration policy led to increased difficulty in obtaining visas and increased time necessary for processing visas. These delays and obstructions forced universities to host functions and offer programs abroad (Witt, 2008).

In some cases, and perhaps increasingly, the traditional US university role of providing local economic development assistance now encompasses assistance for local constituents to tap into the global marketplace. In addition, though sometimes controversial, local outreach efforts are often accompanied by global outreach goals. Besides developing global awareness in graduates through study abroad experience, US institutions face domestic pressure to develop programs abroad that can serve as a gateway to economic development for US companies in various regions around the globe.

Development of US International Programs within the Global Marketplace

The US system of higher education has always functioned at least partially as a market, with institutions vying for faculty, students, funding, reputation, and research dollars. Kerr and Gade characterize the American system as a "gift of history" with responsiveness to the market a fundamental social institution in the American system from the beginning (qtd in Gürlz, 2008, p. 55). However, according to Newman, Couturier and Scurry, the competition of the previous decades was largely benign. Today, it is more severe as the basic nature of the US higher education system is changing (2004).

Previously, US universities and colleges were accustomed to an established place in their segment of higher education and in their geographic area. Newman et al. claim that states operated what were basically cartels of public institutions where three-quarters of the college students in the US were enrolled (2004, p. 9). Now, competition crosses these boundaries. Universities must compete against new providers for students from within their geographic region (Afolayan & Witt, 2010) and must compete for international students with the whole world (Altbach, 2004a).

Moreover, changes in the perceptions and resulting policies affecting higher education have forced US universities to enter the market in order to bridge resulting budget gaps. For example, with the election of Ronald Reagan in 1980, education became increasingly budget driven, increasingly viewed not as a public good or as a source of public service, but as a drain on public funds. Reagan implemented large scale cuts in education funding, reducing the budget in the Fiscal Year 1981 and 1982 by 20 percent (Clark & Astuto, 1989, p. 5). The Reagan administration supported the notion that the primary recipient of educational benefit was the individual student, not society. Reagan's "New Federalism" shifted funding responsibilities to the states and, gradually, to individual students and their families. Since the high tuition/high aid policies did not cover the costs of most students, the burden of funding was shifted to the individual in the form of student loans (Slaughter & Leslie, 1997). Rather than increase federal funding, legislation promoted personal loans as a way to bridge the gap between lagging federal aid to students and the rising costs of higher education (Slaughter & Leslie, 1997). In fact, the reliance on personal loans increased 30% between 1978 and 1994, primarily among students from middle income families (Hannah, 1996, p. 499). This policy reorientation was also significant because it broke with the historic American commitment to promote access to postsecondary education (Hannah, 1996).

With the signing of the Bayh-Dole Act in 1980, research funding, too, was shifted into the market as universities were allowed to retain title to inventions developed through federal funds. This act encouraged academic capitalism through increased competition for potentially lucrative projects. Corporate leaders and politicians worked with heads of universities to shift research away from purely military fields to technology and science projects that would bring additional revenues in the postindustrial age (Slaughter & Leslie, 1997).

Clark and Astuto argue that the Reagan administration's education agenda derived from broader social policy preferences, which included a reduced social program budget, the elimination of regulations, and the corporatization of social programs (1989). "Reaganomics," increased defense spending, reduced education spending and income taxes, and forced US higher education on the defensive while requiring the development of a strict business model. Academic institutions developed mission statements, strategic planning, budget systems, cost-effectiveness analysis and marketing research (Lucas, 1994, p. 238). By shifting higher education institutions further towards the corporate model, the Reagan era laid the groundwork for the development of the education "sector" of global trade for the US.

Newman et al. show that this trend continues. In a reversal from the move towards statewide coordinated systems and governing boards of the 1950s and 1960s, decentralization and deregulation are being encouraged with an "accountability-autonomy" trade-off for institutions (2004, p. 33). State governors have called for postsecondary institutions of education to improve productivity and accountability. Governors and legislations are reported to cite significant problems with higher education, ranging from the failure to address steadily rising costs to a lack of assessment of learning (2004, p. 38).

Clearly, in accord with global trends, market forces have invaded the US academic landscape, affecting all aspects of its functioning. Within the realm of international programming, market ideals of increased brand recognition, revenues, and global labor demands all serve as additional rationales for developing international linkages in higher education.

Development of engineering programs in US higher education.

Perhaps nowhere is evidence of the "conscious use of institutions' use for the selected purpose of the nation-state" (Kerr, 1991, p. 17) more obvious in US higher education than in the discipline of engineering in higher education. As economist and social critic Thorstein Veblen has observed, knowledge inevitably embodies the particular circumstances of its creation. Science "will take its character and its scope and method from the habits of life of the group, from the institutions with which it is bound in a web of give and take" (from Leslie, 1993, p. 9). Yet according to many critics from inside the academy and out, the web of science is a tangled knot of government and industry influence. Collin Tudge argues in *The New Statesman* that

> industry and science are locked in a positive feedback loop ... industry provides the wealth that finances the science that produces the high technologies that enable the industry to make more wealth... but industry cannot afford to be altruistic, as its executives are wont to point out. It cannot finance science that does not increase its own wealth. (2004)

This portrayal of influence and control captures but one strand of what critics have called the triple helix, or golden triangle, of the university, government, industry web.

In the triple helix conception of the relationship between universities, government and industry, universities conducting research are seen as incubators for new knowledge that will lead to patents from which economically beneficial applications will emerge (Kaghan & Barnett, 1997 p. 71; Etzkowitz & Leydesdorff, 1997). William Fulbright called this same relationship the military-industrial-academic complex, a term made more descriptive when we examine engineering programs specifically (Fulbright, 1970). The role of the government helice with regard to US engineering higher education is perhaps most apparent in the form of military contract funding.

Historically, the role of US universities in scientific development was centered on sophisticated federally funded laboratories in the sciences and engineering. Knowledge generated would be disseminated in academic journals and professional conferences without specific links to industry (Jantsch, 1972). Yet Stuart Leslie persuasively demonstrates that, in many disciplines, particularly engineering, the US military set the paradigm for American science (1993). Just as the technologies of empire such as submarine telegraphy and steam power had defined the relevant research programs for Victorian scientists and engineers, so the military-driven technologies of the Cold War defined the critical problems for the postwar generation of American scientists and engineers.

> Indeed, those technologies virtually redefined what it meant to be an engineer – a knowledge of microwave electronics and radar systems rather than alternating current theory and electric power networks; of ballistic missiles and inertial guidance rather than commercial aircraft and instrument landing systems; of nuclear reactors, microwave acoustic-delay lines, and high powered traveling wave tubes rather than generators, and X-ray tubes. These new challenges defined what engineers studied, what they designed and built, where they went to work, and what they did when they got there. (Leslie, 1993, p. 9)

Leslie traces the impact of the US military on American science by following the influx of funding that came to dominate engineering higher education budgets. During the WWII period, spending for defense related research climbed to fifty times that of prewar levels. By the 1950s, Department of Defense (DOD) accounted for 80 percent of the federal R&D budget. As DOD spending decreased through the 1970s and 1980s, the National Science Foundation, the National Aeronautics and Space Administration and the National Institutes of Health took over as sources of military R&D funding (Leslie, 1993, p. 1). Prior to WWII, military research and development spending absorbed on average less than 1 percent of total major power military expenditures. By the 1980s, the R&D share of military spending had increased to 11-13 percent (Paarlberg, 2004, p. 123). It was in this period that the US took the scientific as well as the industrial lead through expenditures to its universities.

President Eisenhower presided over much of the Cold War entrenchment of military funding into higher education. His famous farewell address pointedly identified the "grave implications" of the "military-industrial complex" as a threat to political and intellectual freedom. He presaged that the government contract could become "a substitute for intellectual curiosity." Further, he warned that the threat "of domination of the nation's scholars by Federal employment, project allocations, and the power of money is ever present" (Schiller & Phillips, 1970).

According to Feldman, President Eisenhower's fears have been realized (1989). Relying on data from the DOD, Feldman shows dramatic increases in military funding for many engineering universities in the 1980s. For example, between 1982 and 1986, military funding increased by 40% for the University of Michigan, by 47% at MIT, and by 46% at the University of Illinois. Such dramatic increases were not one time aberrations, but instead illustrate trends that have continued, and have even been surpassed. For example, after the September 11th attacks, total federal R&D outlays were up to $112 billion, roughly 20 percent in real dollars above the earlier Reagan-era peaks (Paarlberg, 2004, p. 131). By 2003, the US was spending roughly as much on the weapons development component of its military budget as any other single nation state was spending on its entire military budget (Paarlberg, 2004, p. 132).

While cash-strapped universities were eager to have funding, many critics have consequently built on President Eisenhower's dark predictions for the effects of such a boon. Feldman finds that the military is able to wield political influence through the academic sponsorship that not only covers research costs, but often laboratories and administrative overhead (Feldman, 1989). With the increased dependency on military funding comes a

> greater tendency to fall in step behind the military's objectives in science policy ... by thinking in terms of what research would be of interest to, and hence funded by, the DOD. Such dependency could also shape the political orientations of faculty affecting what questions they ask and do not ask of their benefactors. (Feldman, 1989, p. 234)

Similarly, Dumas has argued that the attraction of military research and development dollars directs faculty creative thinking along lines different from those that might otherwise be followed. Research tends to be skewed to follow technological pathways of greatest interest and relevance to the military, or with results that might generate spin-off projects of military interest (1984, p. 129).

Further, graduate students will be influenced by the ongoing research projects of their sponsoring faculty and the projects under way at their institution. Since the nature of work performed at the early stage of career tends to create long-term trajectory and to shape graduate student thinking, as well as careers, such exposure to military-oriented objectives may carry long term effects (Dumas, 1984, p. 131). Dumas traces the early impact of the "brain drain" of scientists and engineers away from civilian-oriented industry to technologies and discoveries directly motivated by the military serving part of industry. In the mid-1980s, he found that nearly 40 percent of the nation's engineers and scientists were engaged in military-industrial operations.

> Since 38 percent or more of America's engineers and scientists have been seeking military-oriented solutions to military problems for the past several decades, it should be no surprise that the development of military technology has proceeded at a rapid pace in the US. (Dumas, 1984, p. 143)

Yet, he laments that the civilian oriented technology had necessarily suffered a corresponding retardation due to the devotion of so much engineering and science talent dedicated to US military goals.

This argument takes on even greater significance when we place it within the current global network of higher education. As previously stated, the US attracts the largest number of engineering students from around the globe (Zakaria, 2008). Research on the effects of "brain drain" typically focus on the benefits in the form of increased numbers and diversity among engineers, or the remunerations and investments made possible to the country of origin (Lucas, 2001), and even the technological transfer that may benefit countries of origin (Lucas, 2001; Kapur, 2007). Yet what has received much less consideration is the impact of US national goals on this international assemblage of students. Since US engineering programs are drawing the best and brightest minds from around the globe, those students then necessarily become subject to the influences within US engineering education programs. Whether these internationally recruited students stay in the US or return to their own country upon graduation, much of the direction of engineering education and consequently the likely direction of research has been influenced by US national goals. The possibility of corresponding retardation in civilian oriented technology is then likely further magnified beyond US borders. While previous studies have considered the dominance of first world issues over third world concerns in the networks of science, the perspective made possible by this book illuminates the contributing effects that world-class nationally dominated engineering programs play in defining engineering education, and then consequently, altering the directions of future engineering practice.

Moreover, many scientists have argued that defense sponsorship of university research has a direct impact on the political stances taken by academic scientists (see Leslie, 1993). In fact, other disciplines outside of the sciences have looked to fields of engineering as examples not to follow with regard to risks of DOD funding and the potential for militarization of research (Gonzalez, 2007).

According to Paarlberg, "US scientific prowess has become the deep foundation of US military hegemony. US weapons systems currently dominate because they incorporate powerful technologies available only from scientifically dominant US laboratories" (2004, p. 122). It is the international dominance of the US in fields of science and technology that has made possible the US military dominance.

Yet, Dumas reminds us that there are positive effects of technological innovations developed originally with military purpose and funding. However, he cautions that as a highly authoritarian system, the inherent values of the DOD are at odds with the principles of personal freedom, individuality and pursuit of enlightened self-interest, "the ideals of the wider body of society in the US" (1984, p. 145). Therefore care must be taken when applying such technologies in the civilian sphere to avoid "subtle corruption" and militarization within society as a whole (1984, p. 146).

Leslie argues that the "golden triangle" of research universities, military agencies and high technology industry created a new kind of postwar science that blurred the traditional distinctions between "science and engineering, civilian and military, and classified and unclassified, one that owed its character as well as its contracts to the national security state" (1993, p. 2). Fulbright famously lamented that the "universities might have formed an effective counterweight to the military-industrial complex by strengthening their emphasis on the traditional values of our democracy, but many of our leading universities have instead joined the monolith, adding greatly to its power and influence" (Schiller & Phillips, 1970).

What Leslie, Feldman, Dumas, and others have shown is that the threat of corruption resides both in where the funding was coming from, as well as in where it was going. Not only are there risks that federal defense funding might dampen the intellectual spirit, but also that such funding could corrupt it. Further, these dangers are not limited to DOD funding. The golden triangle has three prongs, with both government and industry tied to universities. Similar issues and criticisms have arisen with regard to technology transfer from universities to industry partners (Jantsch, 1972; Harding et al., 2007). What Leslie (1993) building on Dumas (1984) has demonstrated is that "the nature of the technological pathways explored is a matter of social choice, ... therefore the social context in which technological development proceeds must shape that choice" (Dumas, 1984, p. 145). As Peters explains, "science and technology are constituted through and by social, economic, and political forces" (2006, p. 227).

This context is an important precursor to this study in which the triple helix becomes disrupted by another outside source of funding for US engineering research universities. If engineering education has been so commanded by the military through the influence of funding, then we have to wonder at the effects of this new source of funding. Moreover, if engineering education functions as a manifestation of social context, then new social contexts can be expected to alter the direction and focus of advancements. Because US engineering education programs have fundamentally fueled the scientific advances necessary to dominate the world's most powerful military power, the future directional flow of this originative power is worth tracking. Whether this outside funding source allows for a resurgence of intellectual curiosity and an uncorrupted pursuit of knowledge in the sciences, or instead, becomes another source of domination or potential corruption will be considered. At any rate, it seems clear that the "golden triangle" of military agencies, high technology industry, and research universities has become more complex, with the triangle replaced by a complex web of "multi-locational global networks" (Castells, 2009, p. 129).

Singapore's Higher Education Cultural Framing

Singapore is a compact, densely urbanized city-state in Southeast Asia with over 7,000 persons per square kilometer. Ethnically diverse, multilingual and multi-religious, the population is 76 percent Chinese, 15 percent Malay and 7 percent Indian and European. The dominant language remains English though Mandarin, Malay and Tamil are widely spoken.

Since independence from Great Britain in 1959, and Malaysia in 1965, Singapore is known worldwide for its economic development trajectory taking it from a backwater colonial outpost with low value added manufacturing-based export status to a high value added manufacturing global city status in the dizzying span of a few decades. In this very brief time span, Singaporeans have achieved an eightfold increase in wealth, going from a relatively poor country to one of the world's richest (Horsky & Ghim-Lian Chew, 2004, p. 247).

This process has been guided by an authoritarian government controlled by the People's Action Party (PAP) under the leadership of Lee Kuan Yew (1959-90), Goh Chok Tong (1990-2004) and Lee Hsien Loong (2004-present) which has used the state apparatus to achieve a range of social, cultural, political and economic objectives (Olds, 2007). Many of these directives have impacted the higher education landscape in Singapore. The government views education, and specifically higher education, "as a major route for the country to maintain a competitive advantage and invests large amounts to implement and monitor new education policy" (Horsky & Ghim-Lian Chew, 2004, p. 247). As Horsky and Ghim-Lian Chew point out, "the education system has always been the handmaiden to the nation's goals: first, to sustain economic development and second, to establish national identity" (p. 246).

Governmental power is held firmly in the hands of the elected People's Action Party with opposition parties legal, yet weak and inconsequential (Horsky & Ghim-Lian Chew, 2004, p. 246). Sidhu argues that the Singaporean government has maintained strong authority through its "pastoral care" of citizens (2006). For the Singaporean government, globalization is viewed from the vantage point of the rapid growth of its neighbors, China and India, two mammoth rivals that have obliterated Singapore's earlier lead and reliance on manufacturing. Consequently, Singapore has enacted a slew of policies to steer the creation of a knowledge based economy (KBE) for the city-state. With First World living standards and a seemingly capable and financially astute government at the helm, Singaporeans will likely continue to support directives aimed at preserving growth in the global knowledge economy (Sidhu, 2006, p. 237).

Of interest to our present case is the way in which the Singaporean government interacts with influences from the West. In particular, this case explores the Singaporean government's strategic appropriation of Western modes aimed at economic advancement. Sidhu argues that "seeking to appropriate Western knowledge and practices has never been a problem for Singapore as long as it contributes to the national project of attaining economic success as a capitalist, free-market powerhouse" (2006, p. 243; Olds & Thrift, 2005).

One obvious example of such appropriation aimed at moving the city-state toward a knowledge based economy (KBE) is the adoption of English as the language of Singapore. After notable divisions in social mobility and class between the English-educated and the non-English educated and the resulting widespread unrest (Sidhu, 2006, p. 235), the Singaporean government determined that English was to be the medium of instruction in all schools, and the other three official mother tongues, Chinese, Malay, and Tamil, were to be taught as second languages. The government argued successfully for English because of its use in the world of business, science and technology (Hill & Lian, 1995). From then on, what had been the "native tongue of the colonial master became indigenized as a national language of Singapore" (Koh, 2004, p. 337).[2] Singapore's adoption of the colonially imposed language may seem startling, yet it illustrates a tactical adoption of Western modalities, a strategy Singapore consistently uses to accelerate economic development. Of course, English has since been indigenized into what is referred to as "Singlish"; nevertheless, its use has proved to ease Singapore's economic rise. As this case will show, in its brief national history and accelerated economic ascendancy, Singapore has frequently strategically appropriated foreign models.

To further illustrate this point, the historical background of intellectual property law in Singapore provides a vivid example of particular relevance to this study of the Singaporean governments' perceptions of, and reliance on, appropriation to achieve economic aims. In 1985, the US-based International Intellectual Property Alliance report noted that, "Singapore is truly the world capital of [intellectual] piracy" (Uphoff, 1991, p. 13). Uphoff explains that copyright piracy was "a more or less acceptable occupation, and pirates were estimated to control 80-90% of the tape-market" (1991). An estimated $270 million worth of pirated tapes and books were shipped throughout Asia from Singapore in 1984 making Singapore a piracy hub of Asia (Uphoff, 1991). Due to the large amount of popular cultural products from the US, American companies began pressuring the Singaporean government to enforce and reform copyright laws. Singapore boldly argued that it would change its laws when it was in Singapore's interest to do so (Ramcharan, 2006, p. 323). Prime Minister Lee Kuan Yew went so far as to tell a visiting Congresswoman that since the US had allowed Japan to rebuild its economy by copying everything, it could not tell South East Asian countries that they could not do the same (Uphoff, 1991). Ramcharan suggests that Singapore saw itself, and to a large extent was, a developing country and subscribed to dependency theories which viewed IP rights as a means to keep those at the periphery dependent on those at the center (see Ngenda, 2005). The G77, comprised of developing nations, purported such views about IP to the international community (Ramcharan, 322).

Yet in a dramatic turnaround, by 2002 Singapore was rated the most "IP protective" country in Asia by the Political & Economic Risk Consultancy (qtd in Ramcharan, p. 322). Rather than copying tapes and books, Singapore's government shifted to strategically coping and adopting the policies of the West.

Singapore's rapid and stringent adoption of IP protection occurred for several reasons. First, IP was included as a point of discussion during the Uruguay Round of the GATT (Knight, 2003). Without accepting IP protection, Singapore would be severely compromised in trade negotiations. Second, pressure from the US increased as knowledge intensive goods began to occupy a larger share of US exports. This issue was referenced in everything from presidential speeches to less public negotiations centered on IP protection (Uphoff, 1991). Finally, Singapore faced the threat of loss of benefits under the General System of Preferences. After hearings of a Parliamentary Select Committee and a number of consultations with US delegates, the Copyright Act was passed in early 1987.

The shift to a knowledge based economy has spurred the continued enforcement of copyright as a part of the strategic plan. Indeed, copyright industries in Singapore now constitute a significant amount of the national wealth (Ramcharan, p. 332). Here again we see Singapore strategically "copying everything" in order to build its own economy. In this context, similar to Singapore's adoption of English as its native language, the protection of IP is another example of Singapore adopting, even embracing, a foreign transplantation for its own economic advancement. Despite earlier protestations that IP would keep Singapore on the periphery, it is now generally held to be one of the nation's key strengths as a global knowledge hub (Lee, 2008; Ramcharan, 2006).

In addition to the use of English language and the protection of IP, foreign universities have played, and continue to serve, a central role in Singapore's development. Beginning in the mid-1980s economic crisis, education was identified as a service sector worthy of being nurtured for its potential to increase revenues and export earnings (Economic Review Committee, 2002). Kris Olds attributes a number of objectives to Singapore's subsequent reliance on foreign education providers including the diversification of Singapore's labor market, increased competition and synergy between foreign institutions and local institutions, and ultimately, Singapore's emergence as a knowledge hub with significant university-industry linkages (2007, p. 973). Olds finds that, "foreign institutions are recognized by the Singaporean state as playing a fundamental role in restructuring the economy" with the overall goal of creating a virtuous circle: draw in the best universities with global talent; this talent then creates knowledge and knowledgeable subjects; these knowledgeable subjects, through their actions and networks, then create the professional jobs that drive a vibrant KBE with profitable regional links. (Olds, 2007, p. 973)

From the mid-1980s through the 1990s, Singapore's higher education system experienced the massification drive that continues through the present with an increase of student participation from 5% in 1980 to 21% by 2001 (Olds, 2007, p. 963). This tremendous growth first led Singapore to import higher education from foreign providers. In addition, using attractive salaries and benefits, Singapore recruited foreign faculty to cope with its rapid expansion (Lim, 1995, p. 76).

By the late 1990s, Singapore's stated goal of moving to a knowledge based economy spurred an emphasis on better educated and more skilled citizens armed with creativity to drive future economic development (Lim, 1995). An example is the Singaporean government's 1997 policy initiative, "Thinking Schools, Learning Nation" (TSLN). The new Singaporean curriculum intervention included an emphasis on the teaching of critical thinking and of developing creativity in students. The concept of "thinking schools" entails education institutions developing future citizens capable of engaging in critical and creative thinking, while "learning nation" emphasizes that education is a life-long endeavor (Mok, 2008, p. 531).

By 1998, the Economic Development Board (EDB) launched "WCU" designed to attract 10 world class universities to Singapore within ten years through a variety of linkage mechanisms (Olds, 2007, p. 963). According to the Head Minister for Education, Singapore's goal was to become "the Boston of the East . . . a focal point of creative energy; a hive of intellectual, research, commercial and social activity; a knowledge hub; a confluence of people and idea streams, an incubator for inspiration" (qtd in Olds, 2007, p. 959). Mok delineates three major stages of higher education reforms that were aimed at achieving this goal.

First was the creation of the International Academic Advisory Panel (IAAP), comprised of prominent scholars from international higher education institutions or community leaders from big corporations to help the universities develop into world-class institutions in terms of teaching and research (Ministry of Education Singapore, 2001). Changes in admissions and curriculum were adopted that would lead to greater emphasis on critical thinking skills and creativity (Mok, 2008).

The second stage was the establishment of Singapore's third university by August 2000. The privately owned Singapore Management University (SMU) was formed in collaboration with the Wharton School of Business at the University of Pennsylvania (Mok, 2008, p. 533). This new institution was designed partly to inject a degree of internal competition into Singapore's higher education landscape.

The third stage developed out of overseas study trips to Hong Kong, Canada, the UK and the USA to identify good practices in overseas universities. In exchange for greater autonomy, Singaporean universities were urged to be more responsive in making timely decisions and adjustments in order to achieve excellence. At the same time, the universities had to put in place systems and structures of talent management, organizational process and resource allocation in order to achieve the highest possible value and return on the investment of public funds (Mok, 2008, p. 533).

In order to lure foreign universities to Singapore, the EDB courted universities in R&D rich contexts (Olds, 2007, p. 967). In addition to emphasizing Singapore's cosmopolitan atmosphere, financial incentives were strongly applied. For example, INSEAD received $10 million in research funding over the first four years of its Memorandum of Understanding (MOU), plus soft loans, reduced land values, easier to get to work permits, housing access and other benefits (Olds, 2007, p. 967). Similar arrangements exist with Wharton and were used to attract the now defunct Singaporean campus of the University of New South Wales. While the exact scale of the subsidies is confidential and tied to 4-5 year MOUs and other contractual elements, it is clear that the typical foreign university being courted received several million dollars of direct and indirect subsidy (Olds, 2007, p. 967).

In 2003, building on WCU, Singapore launched Global Schoolhouse, an economically driven initiative marketing Singapore's safe and secure environment. Its three stated goals were to attract the world's most reputable universities as an extension of the 1998 legislation, to align local universities in an entrepreneurial and business mindset, and to recruit increasing numbers of international students (Montsion, 2009, p. 647). To these ends, the government adopted a series of coordinated measures to expand and extend the higher education opportunities. Targeting 150,000 international students by 2015, the EDB was selling vacant property to interested private education institutions with a priority given to business schools (Montsion, 2009, p. 647). In addition, student visas were being fast-tracked for approval. Moreover, many international students are targeted through bonded scholarships requiring students to work in Singapore for three to six years after graduation. As many as 60% of such scholarship recipients make the transition to permanent residents proving the effectiveness of this policy (Montsion, 2009, p. 648). To further entice universities, substantial sums were being allocated into research and development by the government of Singapore through its Science and Technology plan. For example, in 2006, the government announced more than $8.3 million for research and development expenditures during 2006-2010. According to Olds, "a large proportion of this will find its way into research programs focused on biotechnology, water technology, and software engineering" (2007, p. 967).

Olds argues that Singapore has relied on the partnerships between local and foreign institutions to enable local faculty to engage in a learning process with respect to program development, curriculum development, pedagogical practice, and research practice all in a manner that can facilitate the formation of university-industry linkages in the broadest sense (2007, p. 969). In these ways, foreign universities are serving as models of practice, another example of the Singaporean government appropriating Western modalities for economic advancement. The US "golden triangle" of university-government-industry involvement is then exported and incorporated into the Singaporean higher education system.

Similarly, Sidhu states that increased commercialization of new technologies and new industries was a clear goal of the Global Schoolhouse policy (2006, p. 245). For example, "the long experience of Wharton and Carnegie Mellon in strategically facilitating the formation of university-industry linkages in the United States was transferred to Singapore, and has created an important formative legacy" (Olds, 2007, p. 969). Such linkages build on existing and potential connections that local universities already had. Moreover, the foreign institutions used their partnerships with local institutions to extend their own network into Singapore and the broader Asian network. According to Olds, "the logic behind this is to create networks that can be used in the enhancement of the research and teaching process" through the acquisition of research funding, industry feedback, and joint research (Olds, 2007, p. 969). Internships further enhance the foreign university/local university/industry partnership. Also, graduates are able to acquire career placements with associated local and foreign firms. Finally, alumni networks deepen the connections between foreign and local institutions and industry. Olds finds that both foreign and local universities are "intensely strategizing *vis a vis* the creation of the foundations for long-term university-industry linkages in both Singapore and the broader Pacific-Asian region" (2007, p. 970).

Overall, when examining the context of the Singaporean education milieu, it is clear that many facets of US education have been imitated in Singapore's drive for economic growth and repositioning. The golden triangle of government, industry and university that has been a source of controversy in the US has been adopted in Singapore, demonstrating at once the power of US higher education models and at the same time Singapore's reliance on Western models for economic advance. However, in the same way in which English was indigenized to Singlish, there are a number of indigenizations within the Singaporean higher education ecology that make it a unique and distinctive environment.

First, Singapore has long been criticized for infractions to academic freedom. In the humanities and social sciences, restrictions limit exploration or criticism of government policy or social issues (Althbach, 2007; Lim, 1995, p. 76). Second, critics doubt the efficacy of policies aimed at developing creative thinking or teaching about or learning critical thinking and creativity in a hierarchical education structure that favors exams (Lee, 2008; Koh, 2009). Others argue that "creativity will not blossom to its fullest when governmentality is normalized [as it is argued to be] in the Singaporean habitus" (Koh, 2009). The Singaporean government itself has recognized that the exam-oriented education culture seems to preclude the creation of an innovative, creative citizenry, and continually issues policies in an attempt to generate "thinking skills" of problem solving and flexibility (Tan, 2010). Yet, creativity may be one educational goal that cannot be mandated. "Creativity cannot be taught, but it can be killed" (Zhao, 2006, p. 30 qtd in Tan).

Even beyond dictating faculty and curriculum, the Singapore government has played an important role in determining the supply of graduates through restrictions on enrollment and through its own role in the domestic economy (Lim, 1995, p. 80). It has argued that a controlled admission policy is necessary to ensure that there is no mismatch between supply and demand of graduates (Lim, 1995). Besides masterminding the output of graduates, the Singapore government has also actively influenced the career choices of students, encouraging them to enter fields where there is an expected shortage of manpower and to avoid those where a surplus is expected (Lim, 1995, p.

81). However, Lim argues that as society becomes more affluent, the government will be increasingly pressured to temper its "micromanaging style" (1995, p. 81).

Clearly, the appropriation of US academic models has not resulted in the creation of a mirror image any more than America's own appropriation of British and German modalities did over a century ago. Yet, Singapore's pursuit of a US-modeled education hub seems to represent what Sidhu has called "an open acknowledgment by the government of the reciprocal relationships between power and knowledge" (2006, p. 257). The national drive for the US-style instrumental and entrepreneurial focus in higher education suggests the consolidation of America's dominance, if not as the geopolitical and economic power eclipsing the former colonial strength of Britain (Sidhu, 2006), then at least the global dominance of the US higher education system. The nature of collaboration between this former colonial outpost with global knowledge hub aspirations and its mentor, model, institution in the US will be explored in the following case study.

Conclusion

This chapter has outlined a broad overview of the relevant research fields underpinning this case in order to provide the historical, political and cultural context that surrounds the topic. Beginning with a review of the terms globalization and internationalization, it then traced the historical development of global trends in rationales for international programming in higher education from the colonial period, through the period influenced by the market, to the emergent models of today. This case study focuses on one such emergent model developed at research institutions due to rationales based on conceptions tied to the global network of higher education in a global knowledge economy.

As we begin our case study situated in specific institutions, it is important to bear in mind the national ecology for higher education in both of the sites of this study, the US and Singapore. Of course the differences between the educational systems are many, yet both were developed by imitating other national systems and then indigenizing them to local cultural and economic needs. In the US, the German and English models combined with localism to create the system that is emulated throughout the world today. US educators develop international programs within a system that historically emphasized development and is more recently also impacted by market forces. In Singapore, adoption of the English language and IP protection signify Singapore's willingness to appropriate foreign models as a strategy of advancement. Nowhere is this policy more evident than its reliance on foreign institutions to shape and transform its higher education landscape into a global knowledge hub. Singapore has modeled its system on the US, yet operates under authoritarian governmental directives.

The melding of these systems through a multi-institutional partnership will put a federally influenced sector of US higher education in collaboration with an authoritarian system with strong ties to global industry. This qualitative case study will attempt to understand the particular rationales, potentialities, and barriers that specific program planners encounter in such a collaboration. The following chapter will detail the methodological assumptions and procedures used in the research of this case.

Notes

1. According to the American Council on Education, intercultural commonly is used to refer to encounters and interactions between people of different nation-states or diaspora cultures. Multicultural typically describes the interactions between people of diverse cultures or ethnic backgrounds, yet living within one nation or community. In the US, multicultural is generally used to highlight and describe ethnic and racial diversity within the border.

2. For a discussion of the policy challenges surrounding the use of "Singlish," see Horsky & Ghim-Lian Chew, p 253-254.

CHAPTER FOUR

Methodological Challenges in a Cross-cultural Study

To empirically examine the flows of the global network of higher education, this book details a case study of a US Midwestern university and a Singaporean university's planning of a multi-institutional PhD degree in Chemical Engineering. The study starts from the methodological assumption that to investigating a new approach in university internationalization reflecting emergent models of international programs, methodology and procedures should be used that are best designed to understand varying and shifting perspectives of a process. Further, this innovation can best be understood through an exploration of participant perceptions and documents tracing the development of the project. The research will be qualitative since data will be analyzed inductively, emerging as disparate pieces of evidence are collected and reviewed.

The researcher who works with pre-structured categories can only find that which has previously been considered. In this study, however, the objective is to uncover rationales, potentialities, and barriers that may be unexpected and unplanned, even to the participants. Research questions will not be framed by operationalizing variables, but will be formulated to investigate the topic in all its complexity and in context. In particular, the study examines different participant perspectives (Erickson, 1986) of the planning process.

This research is explorative, not evaluative. Not concerned with judging effectiveness or setting standards, instead, this study attempts to portray participant perceptions and complexities. The primary goal is adding knowledge and understanding rather than developing recommendations or policy outcomes.

Through the contracted scope of qualitative case study, this research attempts to capture "the particularity and complexity of a single case" (Stake, 1995). This chapter details the theoretical rationale for using qualitative case study methodology, followed by a discussion of the methods and procedures used.

Theoretical Rationale for Qualitative Methods

In order to understand the interplay between local specificity and the global phenomenon of networks, we will need the close lens of qualitative case study. Geertz explains that

> some things you can best study in localities . . . It is with the . . . study in confined contexts that the megaconcepts with which contemporary social science is afflicted. . . can be given the sort of sensible actuality that makes it possible to think not only realistically and concretely about them, but what is more important, creatively and imaginatively with them (1973, p. 23)

Because of the emphasis on understanding the particular manifestation or expression of larger phenomena within a local context, qualitative case study research provides the ideal means to understand the nature of the collaboration between the international partner institutions. Qualitative case study research seeks "understanding of the complex interrelationships" (Stake, 1995, p. 37). In order to observe the local interaction with globalizing trends, we cannot conduct the study at the level of grand narrative. According to Stake,

> The real business of case study is particularization, not generalization. We take a particular case and come to know it well, not primarily as to how it is different from others, but what it is, what it does. There is emphasis on uniqueness . . . the first emphasis is on understanding the case itself (1995, p. 8)

Moreover, in addition to the emphasis on particularization, there is an incorporation of plurality that is well suited to examining an international partnership that necessarily will involve diverse viewpoints. Again, as Stake has outlined, "the qualitative case researcher tries to preserve the multiple realities, the different and even contradictory views of what is happening" (1995, p.12). According to Erickson, the most distinctive characteristic of qualitative inquiry is its emphasis on interpretation (1986). Such an emphasis is well suited to this study's research questions which are centered on perceptions of participants.

Therefore, to capture the specific way in which global networks flow through the nodes of our study as interpreted by participants, qualitative case study will be used. According to Krathwohl, qualitative methods are extremely useful for exploration (1998, p. 229). As Stake has explained, "the intent of qualitative research is "not necessarily to map and conquer the world, but to sophisticate the beholding of it" (1995). Rather than comparing standard processes, this study is interested in the diversity among perceptions, idiosyncrasies of the participants' perceptions of the process from both sites, and the unique qualities of this program planning process.

While Stake (1995) would argue that a case must be bounded, the nodes on a global network would seem to be anything but. By definition a network is ever expanding and intersecting with boundaries only between those included in the network and those outside of its connections. However, the research for this case follows the argument of Robert Yin (1981) that qualitative case study is viable for study of a contemporary phenomenon in a real-life context with unclear boundaries between the phenomenon and the context. The real-life process of planning a multi-institutional degree is situated within unclear boundaries between the phenomenon of the global network of higher education and the perceptions of the importance of network membership. The planning process itself then becomes the boundary within a shifting context.

As a qualitative case study, interviews constitute a primary form of data collection. Weiss (1994) outlines justifications for a researcher to conduct a qualitative interview study, including describing a process and understanding the interpretation of events. Weiss further states that "interviewing gives us access to the observations of others . . . we can learn about places we have not been and could not go and about settings in which we have not lived. . ." (1994, p. 1).

Qualitative interviews are particularly useful to develop a rich contextual description that incorporates multiple perspectives on the process. Guba and Lincoln distinguish between structured and unstructured interviews. In structured interviews, participants are expected to answer in the terms provided by the interviewer's own framework and definition of the problem based on the researcher's previous research and conception of the problem (Guba & Lincoln, 1981). In contrast, unstructured interviews are "nonstandardized, and the interviewer does not seek normative responses. Rather, the respondent's react to the broad issue raised by the inquirer" (Guba & Lincoln, 1981,

p. 156). Because this is a new program based on emerging rationales, interviews were unstructured and nonstandardized in order to capture multiple perspectives on the process.

Atkinson, Coffey and Delamont (2003) caution that interview participants may create public selves, distorting information gathered in interviews. In what Atkinson, Coffey and Delamont (2003) term our "interview society," participants may construct and act out of created "characters, moral categories, and varieties of experience" that distort reported information (p. 111). However, conducting the interviews as "a conversation between two trusting parties rather than on a formal question and answer session between a researcher and respondent" mitigated any distorting effects of the research method itself (Douglas, 1976).

Moreover, as Atkinson, Coffey and Delamont (2003) explain, interviews rely on the same "culturally shared categories of memory, account, narrative, and experience" as participant observation (p. 110). Therefore interview accounts are "themselves examples of social action [and should be analyzed] in terms of the cultural resources people use to construct them, the kinds of interpersonal organizational functions they fulfill, and the socially distributed forms that they take" (p. 117). The purpose of the study is not to identify the one single truthful account of the planning process, but rather to explore the complexities of the context. Interviews were relied on to provide multiple perspectives of the same phenomenon.

In order to explore such complexities, trust between the researcher and the participants was essential. In this case, factors that aided in establishing that trust included both the longtime personal relationships between participants at the partner institutions as well as the anonymity required by the Institutional Review Board (IRB) at both institutions. Protecting that anonymity was challenging due to cultural differences in institutional governance. At the US institution, for example, most documents regarding the development of the program are public and include the names of participants. At the Singaporean institution, in contrast, most documents were initially internal, and participants were less comfortable with being named directly. By relying on position names, which change frequently and have altered numerous times throughout the planning process of the degree, Singaporean anonymity was protected, IRB requirements were met, yet the research could still maintain validity. While the use of pseudonyms for the institutions themselves admittedly becomes a bit contrived or stilted at times, it was required by IRB standards, and perhaps added yet another veil, though a thin one, of anonymity for participants.

While largely beyond the scope of this study, IRB standards themselves merit study when imposed cross-culturally. In this case, the US institution required extensive IRB procedures including a number of researcher training sessions, a lengthy approval process, and specific data collection procedures. The Singaporean institution required only official notification that such procedures had been followed on the US campus, and that similar standards would be applied for research on the Singaporean campus. According to US IRB staff, the Singaporean institution had modeled its own IRB procedures after the US institution's. This appropriation of US higher education modalities follows patterns that the research itself seeks to study, demonstrating another example of Western isomorphism and the feedback loops that reverberate through higher education and, specifically, at these two sites.

Methods: Research Design

In order to understand the process of development for this collaboration, methods commonly employed in qualitative inquiry, a case study comprised of interviews and document review, were used. This case study focused on interviews of key education directors, administrators and faculty associated with the project on both the US and the Singapore side of planning the joint degree. In addition, documents were analyzed, including key reports, memoranda, reports and meeting minutes from both campuses as available.

Research Setting

This study took place at two locations, a US Midwestern research institution and a Singaporean research institution. Interviews and document collection occurred at both sites.

US institution.

Statistics compiled recently by the office of the Associate Provost for International Affairs at the US Midwestern university demonstrate that the institution ranks near the top in the key metrics of international education: international student enrollment, total number of study abroad students, and the number of federally funded Title VI National Resource Centers for international and area studies.

Specifically, students from over 121 countries study on the Midwestern university's campus; students from that campus study in some 57 countries worldwide; and seven National Resource Centers (NRCs) representing every continent operate there, in addition to one focusing on international business education and research. NRCs support international curriculum development and foreign language programs, foster faculty research, develop international outreach programs, and encourage institutional commitment to international education and research initiatives overall.

The Associate Provost for International Affairs at the US Midwestern university notes that "global competence is a crucial component of a contemporary higher education, and we at [Midwestern university] are committed to assuring that all our graduates will be prepared to function as global leaders and citizens." Taken together, the numbers make clear that this university is a leader in the international education arena.

Moreover, the US Midwestern university is not inexperienced when it comes to forming international partnerships. It maintains 200 active institutional linkages with partners representing more than 50 countries. In 2009, the campus spent over $6 million to support foreign travel and institutional linkages. It maintains 24 formal research linkages in 18 countries, which provide opportunities for faculty and graduate student research across multiple disciplines. The university is also a member of the World Universities Network, connecting research universities internationally through research projects and graduate education partnerships.

In addition to university-wide programs, there are college-based international programs as well. Six foreign language departments, six area studies centers—four National Resource Centers (NRC), and two thematic NRCs, focusing on global studies and international business—complement these programs. In 2005, the university received over $7 million from external sources for international programming.

Finally, the US Midwestern university commits substantial resources to teaching, research, outreach and administration of international programs. One-third of the 3,081 faculty are directly involved in international studies. Salaries for these faculty and administration approximate, respectively, $17 and $10 million. The Midwestern university expended nearly $7 million to support international studies research, foreign travel, and institutional linkages. The university annually spends $3.7 million for library collections in international studies. In 2009, support for international studies totaled nearly $84 million.

Singapore institution.

The international credentials of the Singaporean university are equally impressive. First, the Singaporean university strives to be outward-looking and globally connected in its steadfast pursuit of becoming a leading global university. The university's courses feature a strong global dimension, which is accomplished through overseas student exchanges, attachments and joint teaching programs with some of the world's leading institutions.

Moreover, the Singaporean university is experienced in international collaboration. The university is a member of global consortia that leverage on member universities' diverse and distinctive strengths for excellence in education and research. These consortia provide linkages to hundreds of institutions that span the globe.

In addition to consortia, the university maintains nine international partnerships, many with institutions in the US. Goals of these partnerships range from research to student exchange. In addition to sending high percentages of students abroad, the Singaporean university actively recruits international students, positioning itself as a knowledge hub of the region.

While exact funding numbers are less publicly available at the Singapore site compared with the US site, the demonstrated commitment to international programs is evident in the number and quality of programs offered through the Singapore institution.

Interviews

Since the purpose of this study is to describe a process and to learn how the events in that process have been interpreted, interviews with participants were a primary method of data collection. Selection criteria were based solely on knowledge of the planning process with the goal of including all persons directly associated with the planning of the multi-institutional degree. Through initial contact with the Vice Chancellor for Research at the Midwestern university, participants were recommended and others from both institutions were added through snowball sampling as they became known and agreed to participate (see Tables 1 and 2 below).

Table 1
Participants from Midwestern University

List of Participants
Assistant Dean in the Graduate College
Associate Dean in Student Services
Chair of Campus Senate Committee on Educational Policy
Chair of Graduate College Executive Committee
Chief Legal Counsel
Director of Committee of Institutional Cooperation (CIC)
Director of International Programs
Executive Director of International Research Relations
Former Dean of Engineering
Former Dean of the Graduate College
Former Department Chair of Engineering
Head of Chemical and Biomolecular Research
Professor of Chemical Engineering
Professor of Chemical Engineering
Vice-Chancellor for Research

Table 2
Participants from Singapore University

List of Participants
Deputy President (Research and Technology)
Former Department Chair, Engineering
Former Department Chair, Engineering
International Programs Former Staff Member
International Programs Staff Member
Outside Program Examiner
Professor of Chemical Engineering
Professor of Chemical Engineering
Professor of Electrical Engineering

In this study, interviews were unstructured to allow for the informants to answer from their own frame of reference, rather than from a set of strictly prearranged questions. Though the interviews began with predetermined questions and prompts, they were open-ended and reflective. In addition, prompts and questions were reordered or unused depending on the partici-

pants' responses. Moreover, participants were instructed that they could share additional information and perspectives that they found relevant, making the interviews what Guba and Lincoln call "free flowing" (1981, p. 166). Examples of interview questions and prompts include the following.
1. Tell me about the multi-institutional (joint) degree program.
2. What goals did/do you have for the program?
3. Why that particular partner institution?
4. Describe the planning process.
5. What barriers or constraints have been encountered in the planning process?
6. What could have improved the process of planning?
7. What do you expect to happen next?
8. Was it worth it?
9. What are the expected benefits of this program?
10. How does this program fit in with, or compare to, other international programs run through the department?

Because of the nature of interviews being conducted, it was not possible to "blend into the woodwork," observing others in the natural setting (Douglas, 1976, p. 19). Interviews were conducted primarily in the administrators' or faculty members' offices at a scheduled time. Each participant was interviewed in person for at least one hour. Some follow-up interviews were conducted using SKYPE for participants located in Singapore, though the bulk of follow-up interviews also took place face-to-face. Follow up interviews were only conducted when additional issues were raised by subsequent participants that had not been addressed in the initial interview.

Documents

To triangulate the data gathered in interviews (Stake, 1995), related official and unofficial documents were also a key source for this study. According to Guba and Lincoln, documents "are a stable, rich, and rewarding resource . . . and thus lend stability to further inquiry" (1981, p. 232). In conjunction with the data gathered from interviews, document analysis aided in "coming to know the particularity of the case" (Stake, 1995, p. 39).

On the US side of the proposed program, the study includes a number of relevant documents detailing the institutional process. In addition to promotional materials available from the chemical engineering department regarding the joint degree program, the study includes publicly available meeting minutes concerning the proposed program from the Senate committee on Educational Policy from 2001 through the approval. Relevant annual reports were included as well. Further, the research includes the original proposal itself. Moreover, participants provided memoranda and email text to further supplement document collection.

On the Singapore side of the proposed program, fewer campus documents are publicly available. Nevertheless, Singaporean participants provided me with reports, summaries, program proposals, internal documents, memoranda as well as some email text to supplement data collection.

Data Analysis

Interview data and documents were analyzed qualitatively. Rather than quantifying responses or occurrences based on predetermined variables, the data was inductively reviewed to discover new interpretations or observations. Following the research questions, the information gathered through interviews and documents was reviewed on a thematic basis.

After reviewing the data, information was categorized into three general categories of rationales, barrier, and potentialities. Then, a rough timeline of program development was made in order to capture shifts in perceptions over time. In this way, we are able to observe shifting perceptions in each of the general themes through the process of developing the degree program.

Conclusion

Through the contracted scope of qualitative case study, this research attempts to capture "the particularity and complexity of a single case" (Stake, 1995). This chapter has detailed the theoretical rationale for using qualitative case study methodology, followed by an explanation of the methods used.

Since the objective of this study is adding an empirical perspective rather than developing recommendations or policy outcomes, qualitative case study allows the attention to specificity through participant perceptions required for this research. This study is primarily explorative, not evaluative. Rather than analyzing effectiveness or setting standards, this study attempts to portray participant perceptions and explore the complexities of the case.

In the following chapter, we trace the narrative of program development through the interviews and documents collected in this study.

CHAPTER FIVE

Building a Global Alliance

Introduction

Utilizing information obtained from interviews and pertinent documents, the purpose of this chapter is to provide the context, initial perspectives, and the original formulation of objectives of the program planners as they began and then progressed through the initial stages in the development of the international multi-institutional degree. The following narrative thus provides an overview of participants' perceptions of the historical, economic, and cultural issues that surrounded the original alliance. Further, the chapter traces the development of the relationship as the partnership takes root, detailing the initial goals that participants had for the development of the alliance. Even from the earliest stages, local rationales and global possibilities begin to collide with cultural barriers for the participants.

Data on this historical context specifically illuminates two of the key themes analyzed in this research. First, on both sides of the partnership, local economic changes occurred that encouraged participants to pursue partnerships abroad. Though the local impetus varied substantially between the partners, the global network of higher education makes the alliance of institutions a potential solution to very different local problems. Moreover, shifting perceptions of globalization and growing recognition of the global network in higher education leads administrators and faculty on both sides of the original partnership to form this international alliance. Though the local issues were quiet disparate, almost opposite, shared interpretations of the importance of global network membership unite the participants despite the oceans, issues, and even hierarchical arrangements that divide them. As outlined in chapter three, one of the emerging trends in international education is the strategic alliance of institutions to meet economic goals, particularly in the sciences where the high cost of research encourages collaboration.

Second, interviews and documents reveal that at the inception of the partnership, participants at both the US and the Singaporean institution were shifting their perceptions regarding their own institution's position as a part of the global network, redefining what role their respective institutions should take with regard to this international engagement. Defying the traditional roles the institutions had previously followed in international programming, both institutions chose to develop a new model to reposition their institutions within the global network of higher education. The resulting strategic alliance or collaborative partnership aims to be flatter in hierarchical arrangement compared to the former development models of international programming and allows for the transfer of information that might otherwise have been considered proprietary (Olds, 2007).

Other features of this emerging model distinguish it from the solely market based model. Contrary to what neo-liberal conceptions might lead us to expect, personal relationships as well as both national and local governments all play defining roles in the development of the relationship between the two institutions.

To understand the context of the program planning process, we begin by examining what led participants in the US to engage with the institution in Singapore. Though there were only a few administrators involved at this initial stage, by tracing the footsteps of these US program planners, we can sketch the development of the global network of higher education as it impacts this US institution. The original motivations of international engagement in many ways reflect the typical historical pattern for US universities. For example, the Midwestern university traditionally admitted only a few international students, focusing their mission on geographically local students. With decreased state funding and increased opportunities abroad, administrators gradually began to pursue international students as a potential source of additional revenue.

Moreover, as we explicate the historical development of the program, we can observe the evolution of global perspective among program planners serving as administrators and faculty on the US side of the partnership. Once they begin to engage with the dynamic institution in Singapore, their views regarding their institutions and, by extension, students' and community's place in the world begin to shift. Consequently, they press their colleagues to develop programs and policy that will engage with both local and global demands.

Meanwhile, the partnership development in Singapore highlights the shift from a manufacturing economic and, thus, educational emphasis, in federal and institutional policy toward the current goal of positioning Singapore as a global knowledge hub, with the institution in this case study as a "key node in global knowledge networks" according to internal documents from the Singapore university. These shifting economic demands cause tremendous growth and accompanying change for the Singaporean university. The resulting pressure to recruit global expertise prompts an examination of then current international relationships. Dissatisfaction regarding some of those current partnerships effects a reformulation among Singaporean program planners of their desired role in the global knowledge network and their institution's relative weight in the global network of higher education. Seeking to move beyond their colonial patterns, program planners on the Singapore side use the partnership as a development tool, renegotiating the hierarchical positioning within international engagements.

The reformulation of international partnerships gets reiterated and (re)imagined by the Midwestern university in a feedback loop of policy and practice. The resultant collaboration moves beyond the historical interpretations of international partnerships for both institutions, developing a new paradigm that follows what Castells and other globalization theorists have shown to be a network, with no clear center, shared codes of communication, and pre-eminence of inclusion, with the "power of flows tak[ing] precedence over the flow of power" (2009, p. 500).

The Original Context of the Partnership, Midwestern University

Reflecting the trends noted in the literature on international programs in the US, the initial contact between the Midwestern university and Singapore was made through international students attending the US university. However, in contrast to some critics who suggest that funding is sometimes the chief rationale for recruiting international students (Selingo, 2007; Marginson & Rhoades, 2002: Altbach & Knight, 2007; DeWit, 2002), the high quality of the Singaporean students is what administrators and faculty remember and describe first when asked about their earliest interactions with the Singaporean institution and their initial impressions. The Dean of Engineering at Midwestern university at that time spoke about the important role that high quality students played in the early years of the alliance between the US university and Singapore in general. Even in the climate of shrinking state funding in the late 1980s and early 1990s, the Dean of Engineering from the Midwestern university had come to Singapore following the trail not just of gold, but of bronze. That is, bronze tablet caliber students. According to the former Dean:

> Each year we would get about a dozen undergraduate students from Singapore and four years later, when they gave out awards in April, you would think we were 90% Singaporean. They were expected to get bronze tablet,[1] and they usually did. They were excellent students. Singapore's Economic Development Board (EDB) recruited these scholarship students, the best of the best, and sent students all over the ... Midwest. [The director of the EDB] said, only half jokingly, "I would send them there because there was nothing they could do but study." (personal communication, February 25, 2009)

Though funding becomes more important as the partnership develops, early comments seem to suggest that quality was the initial feature that caused Singaporean students to be attractive to the Midwestern institution. The former department chair of Chemical Engineering has a similar recollection of the initial contact between the department and Singapore in general.

> The EDB sent top students on full scholarship, with a stipend. It was an easy program to support since the students were stellar and well-funded. Faculty had no complaints with that. They were just excellent, really top-notch students, and we had the funds to work with. At first, I knew only the students. I didn't know who EDB was or who its director was. (personal communication, February 29, 2009)

These comments demonstrate that administrators were initially struck by the high academic caliber of the Singaporean students. Yet, in addition to the academic quality of the students, the former Dean of Engineering remembers the financial rewards that came with these particular undergraduates.

> We also would receive a subvention to take care of them, and they needed very little taking care of at all. I was able to invest that funding back into the international program and used it to grow. We did things in Europe, other places. I thought, I better keep going to Singapore. I want more like this, or well, at least I want them to keep coming. (personal communication, February 25, 2009)

Perhaps because of his Princeton background, the Dean of the College of Engineering at that time did not share the traditional Land-grant prejudice against students from out of state or out of country that was typical at that time at many public institutions. Indeed, he remembers noticing the lack of international and out of state students even at his initial interview at the Midwestern university. Then, in 1989, Midwestern university had an international enrollment of less than 10 percent compared to Princeton's 13% (Institute of International Education).

> I remember mentioning to the President at that time the low number of out of state and international students. The President agreed that we needed more, but explained that the state wouldn't stand for it. One of my predecessors was coming [to Singapore] and telling them that we didn't take international students, and we barely did. A few slipped in, but we didn't recruit them back then. The idea was, we can't give up places from state residents to international students, not only from out of state, but people who aren't even citizens. (personal communication, February 25, 2009)

This situation corresponds to the localism inherent in the Land-grant model of research institution. Though top administrators and some faculty disagreed with this insular policy, pressure from policy makers and other local stakeholders kept the university focused on local in-state students.

Defying local pressures for this policy that Midwestern university was primarily if not only for in-state students, and with the support of the President, the former Dean went to Asia, and specifically to Singapore, to recruit more top level students to the College of Engineering. His initial visit led to others.

> I would make a swing, usually Japan, Taiwan, Korea, Singapore, then back to the US, because we had a lot of friends and alumni in the region. Of all of those places, Singapore was the most accessible, a fabulously simple place to get around, no language problems, and just a beautiful city. I always enjoyed those visits. Gradually, I was invited to give some talks, other things, and that's how my coming here started [speaking in Singapore]. (personal communication, February 25, 2009)

This use of international student recruitment as a source of funding mirrors what we have seen in the literature as typical for US institutions at this time. As state funding is cut, universities are forced to look elsewhere to find their own sources of funding to make up shortfalls. International students are one potential source. While criticisms in the literature suggest that universities were entirely motivated by funding, in this case, the high quality of the students combined with the added funding they brought to the engineering program made the Singapore students particularly sought after. Both administrators mentioned that the high quality of the students eased any potential conflicts about the funding received. However, there were conflicts, as we will see later.

After a few recruiting visits to Asia, the Dean of Engineering at Midwestern university had been invited to give lectures and even spend a few weeks as a visiting faculty member at the Singaporean university. This was during a period of enormous growth for the chemical engineering field in Singapore. The former Dean remembered the impact of the tremendous economic developments of this time. He attributed much of this dynamic growth to the charismatic leadership of the EDB. Though the former Director was not available for an interview during data collection, his role in the original formulation and support of the partnership and initial program was discussed and corroborated by several participants. The former Dean described him affectionately.

> He had boundless energy, lived on airplanes, knew everyone worth knowing all over the world, and had a vision for Singapore that was phenomenal. It was like nothing I'd ever seen. The major projects he was undertaking, it was impressive to see. I never knew him not to have some grand vision, and typically accomplished it. (personal communication, February 25, 2009)

Even in these early recollections, the personal relationship between these two key participants is obviously warm and congenial. Throughout the process, the personal relationships continue to spur the partnership on despite many other difficulties.

Beyond developing personal relationships, it is the dramatic growth occurring in Singapore that draws the interest of Midwestern university administrators. In addition to the draw of well-funded, bright students, the attraction of Singapore as a destination increasingly influences the trajectory of events. The former Dean described the development of Jurong Island, a Singaporean chemical processing facility and one of the largest oil refining facilities in the world.

> The EDB took seven clumps of land, shipped in sand from Indonesia, other places, and made it all into one island. The idea was to have everything ready, utilities, everything they would need, for the oil companies. Exxon and Mobile were in. The thinking was we will give them all the support, with outputs going into some other plant, also on Jurong, so we will put it all in one place together. Other refineries require companies to do something else with the bi-products. Jurong was better in that the whole process could be handled in one place. (personal communication, February 25, 2009)

Once Jurong was in operation, the EDB immediately moved to other projects. Contrasted with the budget cuts and financial constraints being felt in the US, and even in other parts of Asia, this spectacular development occurring in Singapore seemed even more stunning to the former Dean and others.

Chemical engineering was only one area of dramatic growth and transformation occurring in Singapore at this time. Tourism was another major industry for Singapore. A similar island development plan was initiated to create the Indonesian island of Bintan into a vacation resort, mainly aimed at Japanese tourists. As the former Dean explains,

> [The Director] wanted me to see Bintan, really just a jungle and some beaches to start with, some foundations of hotels. We went down to the port to go zinging over to Indonesia to this island. We were on our way over there on one of these hydrofoils when I mentioned the idea I'd had about a joint master's degree. I thought we could bring our students over, have a half a dozen from Midwestern and another half a dozen from Singapore, have them take courses, some in the US, some here, let them get some experience in Singapore with the refineries, and then work on site with the MNC's [Multi-National Corporations] that had operations in both Singapore and the US. In his usual way, [The Director] answered, "Good, I'll pay for half." (personal communication, February 25, 2009)

Deciding to begin such a partnership was the first step in what became a very long journey. The former Dean began working on the first steps to arrange the program. Though the EDB had agreed to pay for half, the remaining portion needed to be secured.

> I worked on the MNC's trying to get the funding sorted out. We sold the idea that these students would have experience working here [speaking in Singapore], and in the US, so they would be able to fold right in. Once we got much of the funding in place, we passed it off to [the Department Chair]. He is the one who did all the leg work to get [the joint masters] up and running. (personal communication, February 25, 2009)

Ironically, the former Dean credits the idea and model for this joint program as the working partnerships that Singapore university already had in operation with an international partner institution. However, in order to be viable from the Singapore side of the partnership, the actual program developed into a new model, in fact, very different in some key respects from the programs that served as inspiration.

The alliance between the EDB, Singaporean university and the Midwestern university continued to strengthen. When the EDB Director's son chose to attend Midwestern university, the Director began to visit the US campus more often and to know the departments of engineering and the faculty better. Soon, other members of the engineering department were introduced into the partnership. The Department Chair of Chemical Engineering at that time remembers being invited to a dinner party at the former Dean's house.

> The day of the party, I was sent a large packet of information detailing the EDB, and that included the Director's dossier with a long list of associations and accomplishments. Boards of directors, memberships all over the world. I had never seen anything like it. That was when my wife and I were first introduced to the Singapore model. The Director travels all over the world forming alliances for Singapore, drawing businesses in, MNC's, and he always travels with an entourage. By then [the Director's son] was attending Midwestern university and was in our department, so I swung by the office on the way to dinner, just to check his status. Make sure he was doing well. Of course, he was doing very well as we would expect from any Singaporean student. (personal communication, February 24, 2009)

The former department chair remembers little of that dinner, but said that less than a month later, he received an email from the charismatic director of EDB inviting him and his family to Singapore.

When he asked the Dean about it, the Dean replied, "If you can think of anything that might be good for your department, you should accept the trip." The department chair then wrote a three page email describing how the department might benefit from this alliance, what might be gained from the trip, and how the cooperation might yield results, all written in what he characterized as very carefully worded, even "tortured language." No sooner had he sent the email than right away the answer came back from the Director of the EDB. "Good. Come." (personal communication, February 24, 2009).

The Original Context of the Program, Singapore University

As discussed, the city-state of Singapore is world renowned for vibrant and steady economic growth since its independence in 1965. Rapid economic development in this short period of time required a constant re-structuring of the economy to maintain such fast paced growth in the face of a dynamic global economy. At the beginning of the partnership, Singapore's economy was evolving from an initial concentration on heavy industry-based manufacturing to manufacturing in knowledge-intensive products such as electronics, engineering and chemicals, as well as the provision of financial and banking services (Ramcharan, 2006, p. 317).

By the 1980s, after a decade of rapid industrialization, land was growing scarce on Singapore's mainland. Therefore, various government agencies worked together and decided to join the southern islands to form one colossal island to create more industrial land, aimed specifically at the petrochemical industries. In 1991, Jurong Town Corporation was appointed the agent of the Jurong Island project. JTC planned and coordinated with various government agencies in providing the necessary infrastructure and services to the island. Physical land reclamation began in 1995, and Jurong Island was officially opened on October 14, 2000, by then Prime Minister Goh Chok Tong. From the nearly ten square kilometers of land area of the original seven islands, as of completion of the land reclamation on September 25, 2009, Jurong Island currently had a total land area of over 30 square kilometers. Reclamation was completed twenty years ahead of schedule (Chan, 2009).

As anticipated, Jurong Island became home to leading petrochemical companies. Industry luminaries from across the globe such as BASF, BP, Exxon Mobil, Chevron Oronite, and Sumitomo Chemical established facilities to capitalize on the efficiencies brought by the comprehensive infrastructure and production synergies from this cluster of development for oil, petrochemical and specialty chemicals. By 2009, nearly S$24 billion had been invested in the project by over 80 corporations (Chan, 2009).

With this enormous expansion aimed at the development of the chemical processing industry occurring in the late 1980s and 1990s, it is not surprising that tremendous growth and change were also occurring in the research universities. Faculty in the engineering department at Singapore university had always focused largely on undergraduate education, yet now there was tremendous pressure to develop graduate programs, particularly in Chemical Engineering.

According to Richard Garrett, deputy director at the Observatory on Borderless Higher Education,

> the mid-1980s saw the beginnings of transnational higher education in Singapore. The government was keen to expand access to higher education, but could not grow domestic capacity fast enough. So despite a period of steady cohort decline post-1985, the transnational market in Singapore expanded significantly due to an increase in tertiary participation of the age cohort from 8 percent in 1985 to 15 percent in 1990. Participation now stands at around 45 percent. This massive expansion has only been possible through foreign provision, whether studying abroad or transnational provision. But while transnational activity was viewed as a way to stem study abroad rates and to mentor local institutions, the long-term aim was greater self-sufficiency [for Singaporean institutions]. (2003)

The partnership between Midwestern university and Singapore university developed at the crux of this transition from foreign dependence to self-sufficiency in Singaporean higher education. Noted in chapter three, the Singaporean government actively pursued an American model of higher education and set the goal of attracting US institutions to Singapore to serve as models for development and to spur competition.

As we observe the development of the partnership, we can see the status within the relationship shift, though at the beginning the Singaporean institution took a secondary position to their prospective foreign partner. On his first visit to Singapore, the former US department chair remembers being treated, along with his family, as "very important people." The former chair describes being put up in a luxury hotel, taken on in-depth tours of housing units, schools, factories, and finally, meeting with his counterpart and faculty at Singaporean university.

> What was interesting on my very first visit was the way that the Singaporean university and even the EDB felt it was a big deal. A department chair from [Midwest University] mattered. They felt really third world, very beneath us [at Midwestern university] so I was a big deal. (personal communication, February 24, 2009)

The former Singaporean department chair remembers this time period for the pressure that accompanied it. From the start of the program, the department chair and other faculty cast Midwestern university in a mentoring role as they developed their own programs during this tremendous growth. This kind of reliance is closer to the colonial or development model of international programming outlined in chapter three. However, as the partnership develops, we can trace a shift in this relationship between the institutions.

> We were in a race to develop world-class graduate level education. We would have the work, but we did not have the graduates, or even the program in place to train them. We needed partners to build and expand our degree programs. We had to expand and grow right away. (personal communication, February 23, 2009)

At the same time that foreign expertise was so desperately needed, some administrators and faculty at Singaporean university were dissatisfied with portions of the previous international programs in which their institution had been involved. While they were reluctant to speak about it, or to name specific programs or names, two faculty members and one administrator all similarly described how dissatisfied they had been with some of the international partnerships they had engaged in up to that point. Characterized as a "colonization," two separate faculty members from that time described programs in which Singapore was providing large amounts of funding, yet the students were attending the partner institutions, and not returning to Singapore with the education and training that the nation demanded. "We were not treated as equals — quite the opposite in fact" (personal communication, February 26, 2009).

One former administrator from the international office at Singapore university remembers feeling pressured to accept any terms that were offered from the foreign institution in previous programs. "It was not a negotiation. It was just a colonization. We were not deciding what we wanted. We were taking anything they decided, and we felt we had to do it" (personal communication, February 25, 2009).

The need to move beyond the colonial model is echoed by others from the Singapore institution. Some Chemical Engineering faculty members from that time comment on how they felt about beginning another international partnership with a US university. "We worked with top brand institutions before, but now we wanted to work differently, with more equal terms in the agreement" (personal communication, February 26, 2009).

Looking back, one former Singaporean department chair claims that "a change in the way we partnered was essential because the faculty felt exploited. They would not want to join [the partnership with Midwestern university] if it was the same" (personal communication, February 23, 2009).

On the other side, the former US department chair remembers being "very impressed" with the quality of the faculty at the Singaporean university even at the first meeting. "I was surprised that I knew many of the names [of faculty members]. Some from conferences, some from research. Some had been A-list candidates for positions on our campus, which got my attention." He goes on to characterize the first meetings.

> I was also amazed at what they were doing and what was being expected of them. My colleague's department [in Singapore] was expanding at an extraordinary rate, doubling and then doubling again, with no limit in sight. There was a great sense of urgency, an incredible race to supply Jurong [chemical processing facility]. They needed a world class graduate program, and they needed it now. (personal communication, February 24, 2009)

In fact, internal review documents from the mid-to late 1990s show that the number of students accepted into Chemical Engineering nearly doubled from 110 to 200 in one year. Moreover, sixteen new faculty positions had been added to the staff of 34. In addition, a new building was being constructed to facilitate research and teaching. This enormous growth and financial investment was in stark contrast to the tight budgets being experienced on the US campus.

The former US department chair admits to being "very caught up" with what he termed the energy and dynamic growth happening in Singapore. "For months after that first visit, my wife and I would think, "well this is how Singapore is doing it. How can we apply this here [in the US or on the Midwestern campus]?" (personal communication, February 24, 2009).

The Chair of the Faculty Senate Committee on Education Policy at Midwestern university also remembers the growth that Singapore university was experiencing and the opportunities that the partnership seemed to offer. He remembers the strength of the facilities as a driving force in the development of the master's degree. "The strength of the Chem E. department was part of it, but the facilities stood out. The research facilities were very impressive" (personal communication, April 28, 2009).

The Chair also spoke of the dynamic economy and the national emphasis on education which made the partnership attractive and intriguing to US faculty and administrators who did not feel that level of government support at their own campus. "Singapore is doing all the right things. They are putting money into research, faculty, and graduate education. They are world-class in that respect" (personal communication, April 28, 2009).

Interviews make clear that at the beginning of the program development, no one on either campus would have considered the two institutions to be equal. Faculty and administrators at Singapore university initially take a deferential role toward their potential US partner, and the US faculty and administrators are surprised by the quality they see in the Singapore department. In addition to the growing affinity between the program planners at the institutions, what seems to drive the relationship is Singapore's enormous need and potential for growth. All participants agree that Singapore and its partners from the West must move beyond its colonial patterns of behavior and develop new paradigms for its developing role in the global knowledge economy. As we saw, US institutions have historically played a development role in their programs abroad, making Midwestern university a reasonable partner for this undertaking. Yet an emerging model is required to move the institutional partnership forward as Singapore faculty and administrators are no longer comfortable in what they feel is a colonial pattern of collaboration.

Development of the Joint Master's Degree

As the working relationship between US administrators and the administrators and faculty at Singapore developed, the details of the proposed partnership began to take shape. The former Dean and the EDB had secured much of the necessary funding. Now, the department chair was left with the difficult task of convincing other US administrators, faculty, and students that the program was valid and worth pursuing. While programs with an international component or even with an international partner had been done before in the engineering department and on campus, this program was unique for the Midwestern university both in its design and in the goal of jointly awarding the masters degree from both institutions. For the Singaporean university, this program represented a different version of the kind of program they already had run successfully many times. The challenge for the Singaporean side was to make this partnership function with greater equality.

The former Department Chair at Midwestern university articulated three main reasons that he wanted to pursue the partnership with Singapore university. First, he explained that he felt strongly that undergraduate students needed to know that there is a world outside [the state].

> In order for the students to be exposed to the ideas of the outside world, Midwestern university would have to have faculty with a global perspective. This would best be achieved if faculty were engaged in research with institutions abroad, working on research internationally. We are, after all, a research institution, so our research has to be global if anything is to be global. (personal communication, February 24, 2009)

Institutions in the US are increasingly pressured by outside stakeholders as well as students and their parents to provide a "global perspective" for students to prepare them for the global economy.

The former Department Chair's second reason related to the constituents outside the university, the corporations and even the local farmers that, in a globalized economy, would require international access themselves.

> We have a responsibility to the economy, to grow the economy by being where the markets are. They aren't in Detroit. Much of our funding comes from corporations in addition to the public money, so following an economic development model, we have to help our customer by playing abroad. We have to help the private sector be in the market by being where the market is. Even farmers are remarkably globally minded. They know that whether it rains or not in Argentina it is going to affect them very directly, but of course, on the other hand, farming requires a very close

attention to the local, so we have to be there as a means to see that the rest of the world matters. (personal communication, February 24, 2009)

His third reason ultimately becomes the most challenging rationale to validate for the campus community as we will see further in chapter six. Similar to the discussion in chapter two of the preeminence of global network membership, the former Department Chair pursued the joint degree with Singapore because he felt strongly that to be a part of the global knowledge network required this partnership. It is within this reasoning that we can see the "power of flows taking precedence over the flow of power" (Castells, 2009, p. 501).

> If we are not there, we are nowhere. A leading education and research institution must attract the best. We must be at the top of mind. We don't do that by sitting in the middle of cornfields. We must solve problems, global problems. Students must recognize and work on problems of the world. We must expand our global footprint and just be out there. We must be top of mind more often and that only happens by extending ourselves. (personal communication, February 24, 2009)

The program that the Former Dean and Department chair had conceived with their colleagues in Singapore did require that the institution "extend itself." Imagined as a new model, it required that the institution develop a new form of international engagement. Moving beyond its role as "benefactor" to a developing institution, this program would require equal footing, with both institutions appearing equally on the scroll that students receive upon graduation. This model represented a new kind of institutional collaboration, an emerging model that would hold vestiges of the development model and market based competition, but would also represent a more equal collaboration involving shared codes of communication and shared responsibility for the degree program.

Indeed, it is clear from the design of the master's program that it was not only intended to provide students with a greater international dimension to their chemical engineering program, but also to rely heavily on a cohort collaboration that is unique for this type of international degree program. Interviews with initial participants credit the global perspective gained through visits to Singapore for envisioning this model. "It became painfully obvious to me that our students desperately needed to work on this kind of global team" (personal communication, February 24, 2009).

Designed for five or six students from Midwestern university and an equal number of students from Singapore university, the program was set to begin in Singapore from July to November.

> Participating students at the host institution are expected to help visiting students with settling-in and orientation. During the first semester, students take courses and prepare for the internship project. The internship in Singapore starts in December and lasts through April of the following year. All the students then relocate to the US and work on the second internship project from May until August. Afterward, they spend the fall semester at Midwestern university, completing coursework requirements. (Internal document, Singapore university, 1998)

The program thus required students to spend equal time at both institutions, with students changing roles between host and guest. Students were paired for the internship portion as well, with one student from Singapore and one student from the US assigned to each internship site (personal communication, February 24, 2009).

The outside examiner of the program was required to review the course materials, observe courses, visit and interview managers at the internship sites and overall, evaluate the joint master's program. This complete review was performed every six months. The outside reviewer stated that:

> in my opinion, this was an excellent program. The camaraderie that developed between the students, in the cohort and in the partnerships, was a key feature that is missing in many programs. In terms of creating a truly international team collaboration that students may encounter in the workforce, this program was tops. The quality of the courses, the internships, it was just excellent. The only problem was in the diploma. We [at Singapore] were expecting a jointly awarded degree, but there was some trouble getting that approved at the US campus. We had to start with separate degrees being awarded, but that wasn't what we had advertised, or what the students wanted. Eventually we got that worked out, but in the meantime, there was some disappointment. (personal communication, February 25, 2009)

When asked why the program had been pursued as a joint degree, which was new to Midwestern university instead of as a transfer program, an off campus program, a dual degree, or other more familiar model, the key administrators involved with that decision had several answers. The Director for International Partnerships at Midwestern university explained that at first, a dual degree program seemed the most likely option. In fact, they ran the initial phase of the joint master's degree as a dual degree program. That is, the students who completed the program received one degree from each institution. However, the administrators were not satisfied with that solution since it meant students received two degrees for completing one program of study. Also, they felt that students on the Singapore side of the program had been dissatisfied with receiving two different degrees (personal communication, January 26, 2009). The former Department chair agreed with but also added to that explanation.

> We had to create a new model. We had to break with what had been done before. We didn't want anything that smacked of inequality. We needed to show that both partners [institutions] were equal. We just could not have the kind of program that had been run before. [Unequal programs of the past] had really sullied the nest [in Singapore]. We wanted the final degree to reflect what the program was – it was a joint master's degree with both institutions participating in all aspects of the program equally. (personal communication, February 25, 2009)

This rationale was very clear to top administrators who had spent time visiting Singapore and working closely with colleagues there. However, the idea of putting Midwestern university's name on a diploma with another institution was treated as a radical concept on the US campus.

The Director of International Research Partnerships remarked that, "looking back, it may have been too idealistic, this multi-institutional degree, but we wanted to show a true collaboration, more than had been done before, because that is what it was" (personal communication, March 12, 2009).

Partially in response to criticism about the proposed joint degree, the former Department Chair planned a mini-conference for faculty from Midwestern university to visit Singapore and meet their colleagues there face to face.

> I brought six or eight faculty to Singapore for our first ever Globalization of Research conference. It started out a disaster. We all met in the large conference room with the idea that we would each give 10 to 15 minute presentations on our research, first one from Singapore, then one from US and so on. The room was hot, the [US] faculty were jet lagged and sleeping. The Singapore faculty were jaded and bored — jobs had been leaving Singapore to China, India, so they knew they had to move to a knowledge based economy. They had built Biopolis, just to show they could make a major research center out of air, and now they had to become a world class research institution and do it now. They had Jurong on line, and it brought enormous expectations. We drug through that long meeting and then we went down to Clark Quay, to some Indian restaurant, and over curry and some pitchers of beer, it all fell into place. We began to complain about not enough money for research, bureaucracies, and all of it, and realized we had much more in common than we thought. (personal communication, February 24, 2009)

Two Singaporean faculty who attended this initial conference gave a slightly different report from the US Department chair's version of the mood of the first meeting, but the overall sense of "relationship building" is captured in each account.

> I was very impressed that they came. Many from the department, and gave research presentations to us, and listened to us. We spent time just talking and planning how our programs could work, what might work for us. (personal communication, February 26, 2009)

> I think of the time when a large number of the faculty came, and we had a conference together. Of course, we had met at conferences before, but this was just for our departments. We felt included in the planning, and we were becoming colleagues together, working together on what we wanted to do. We sat in the conference room and matched up our research interests and areas. Some work was later published out of that and I think, I don't know, but I think some of it may still be going between some of them. Besides just working on the degree, but working together on research too. (personal communication, February 23, 2009)

Despite the mixed feelings reported among participants regarding the mini-conference, administrators from both campuses agreed that forming a close relationship between the departments was essential. The Chair of the Faculty Senate Executive Committee at the Midwestern university emphasized the importance of this relationship.

> At a university like [Midwestern], you have to have cooperation at the unit level. You aren't going to have the Chancellor saying, "I want this joint degree," or "I want this department to work with that university." That just isn't going to happen at a world-class university. You won't get that from a Dean either. It will come about because the faculty are working together and driving it, as it was in this case. A lot of institutions are very interested in collaborating with us, but my response is always, "you have to work with your colleagues at [Midwestern] first." It doesn't happen at the university or college level. The key is that the faculty at the two units must work together. I certainly would not have felt comfortable if these two departments did not have a history. Not administrators either, but faculty. That is the one key. Not just willingness, but eagerness. Eagerness on the part of the faculty. (personal communication, April 28, 2009)

Administrators from the US university stress the importance of that working relationship on the Midwestern side and explained that a jointly awarded degree program signifies that collaborative relationship. According to a former Assistant Dean in the Graduate School at Midwestern university, it shows a true collaboration. When you have a degree program that is jointly offered, it shows an equal amount of control. In the case of a program centered only on transfer credit, for example, it suggests only a cursory approval of the courses, but a jointly awarded degree shows collaboration all the way through the degree process on courses, research, all of it. (personal communication, April 22, 2009)

However, the former Assistant Dean in the Graduate School at Midwestern university remembers the idea of a joint degree as being very problematic.

Accepting transfer credit, working on programs internationally that way, is much, much easier to negotiate. We didn't talk about 'Brand' that much in those days when this program was first being put together, but we still thought about it. We still thought all the time about the reputation of the university and did not want to be seen doing something that would not fit with the brand. (personal communication, April 22, 2009)

Concerns over brand show that some administrators and faculty at Midwestern university were viewing the potential partnership primarily from the standpoint of the market based model of international programming. As we will see in chapter six, the challenges of creating the multi-institutional degree, particularly around issues of what comes to be termed the "university brand," continue to thwart the efforts of participants for years to come.

In the meantime, as the Singaporean students continued to come, and the developing program began to receive some public attention, the repercussions for that internationalization effort were being felt. US chemical engineering faculty members remember resistance among legislatures, in the local papers, and even other faculty who felt that in-state students were being cut out in favor of international students (personal communication, March 13, 2009). The former department chair remembers people accusing Midwestern university of selling degrees (personal communication, February 24, 2009). In at least one case, the former chair remembers a threatened lawsuit finally settled out of court on the Singapore side.

It was clear to me even at this stage that the ideas are deeply, deeply cultural. The history of the campus is tied very deeply to the name of the institution, the brand. From the beginning there was tremendous fear amongst colleagues that we were selling our souls. The Senate Executive Committee reamed us again and again. Look, the [US] system is not designed to be flexible in thinking, no willingness to do something new, unwilling to say yes or no or even to identify the issues. It was very painful, and it speaks volumes about the system in the US. By not changing, it has survived in structure for hundreds of years, but will that same unchanging inflexibility keep it from surviving the next hundreds of years? (personal communication, February 24, 2009)

Echoing the recognition of the institution's resistance to change, the former Dean writes that "permanence is not synonymous with excellence. Unless universities embrace globalization as a new opportunity, they will within a generation, find themselves among the also-rans of the world's research universities" (personal communication, February 25, 2009).

Conclusion

The narrative presented in this chapter traces the initial ecologies, perceptions and motivations of participants as they embarked on the international partnership. As we have seen, the US institution engaged with the Singaporean institution in order to attract excellent, well-funded students. When administrators from Midwestern university saw the facilities that were under construction in Singapore as well as the strength of the Singaporean faculty, the alliance developed further as a means to provide students with an international perspective and internship opportunities abroad. In addition, the dramatic growth of the petrol-chemical industry in Singapore, in contrast to ongoing budget cuts at the Midwestern campus, hinted at future opportunities for the Midwestern university. For the Singaporean university, the Midwestern university first represented a site to train high achieving students through world-class education. The partnership with Midwestern university becomes an opportunity to work with a high ranking US institution while developing their own program and capacity. The collaboration aids in managing the tremendous growth that developing chemical industries are effecting. Despite this widely disparate local impetus, both institutions seek an international partnership to meet local goals, demonstrating even in the early stages of the partnership that for higher education, both the drive to engage globally and the effects of globalization are local.

This narrative has also demonstrated that both sides of the partnership choose to break with traditional international engagement forms typical of their institutions in order to (re)imagine and (re)position their institutions within the global network of higher education. For the Singaporean institution, this partnership provides a new beginning in which the program evolves on more equal footing, with both campuses providing equal parts instruction and mentoring of students. For the US institution, the struggle to achieve the jointly awarded degree represents a greater level of collaboration with an international partner institution on a degree program, with a tacit acceptance of a non-hierarchal position in the international relationship. Within these early stages of the case study, there is no clear privileged center, and both sides of the academic partnership are exercising agency in the push-pull stream of global flows. Of course, this does not render the global network of higher education as flat, without hierarchies. As discussed in chapter two, "the shadow of hierarchy" and "the shadow of the market" (Thompson, 2003) are both traceable in this developing partnership, yet the overriding importance of network membership seems to be a driving force. Rather than dispensing with hierarchal power all together, the case study seems to capture a shift or reformulation of this hierarchy, demonstrating the importance of focusing on "real actors embedded in real places" (Sidhu, 2006, p. 52). While the Singapore institution begins the relationship deferentially, in need of expertise, the tremendous growth in Singapore allows for a repositioning and reformulation of Singapore's role in international engagement. The narrative here suggests that both partner institutions shared the goal of demonstrating membership in the global network of higher education through the degree program and partnership, and through renegotiations of traditional roles, were willing to work as equal partners to achieve that goal.

This narrative also traces the initial stages of some of the barriers that will continue to challenge participants as the international alliance develops further. After only a few years of interaction between the partner institutions, both sides show some frustration with the inability of the US institution to quickly adapt to the new program model. Though barriers of distance and expectations are easier to overcome, the barriers of deeply held cultural beliefs prove more difficult, ultimately effecting "the extent to which societies [localized in this case study to the institutions] will be able to pick and choose the ways in which, and the degree to which they can participate in a global world" (Burbules & Torres, 2000, p. 17). As we will see in the next chapter, these barriers become almost insurmountable and in many ways may limit the potential of the partnership.

Notes

1. The Bronze Tablet is an award for students in the top three percent of the graduating class.

CHAPTER SIX

Barriers to Global Flows in Higher Education

"In the end, it is rather easier to change the world than the university." (Glazer, 1970, p. 82)

As we saw in chapter five, on both sides of the partnership, local economic changes occurred that encouraged participants to pursue partnerships abroad. Though the local impetus varied substantially between the partners, the global network of higher education makes the alliance of institutions a potential solution to diverse, local problems. Moreover, shifting perceptions of globalization and the growing recognition of the global network in higher education lead some administrators and faculty on both sides of the original partnership to forge this international alliance. Shared interpretations of global network membership unite the participants despite the geographical distance, administrative and academic issues, and even perceived hierarchical positions that initially divide them.

Second, interviews and documents reveal that at the inception of the partnership, participants at both the US and the Singaporean institution were refining their acuity regarding their own institution's position as a part of the global network, even redefining what role their respective institutions should take with regard to this international engagement. Defying the traditional roles the institutions had previously followed in international programming, administrators and faculty at both institutions chose to develop a new model to reposition their institutions within the global network of higher education.

Despite the seeming agreement between key administrators at the participant institutions, as we will see in the following narrative and document excerpts, other administrators and faculty members, at the US institution in particular, were far from united in their vision of the institution's participation in this partnership, and the resulting perceived shift in global network membership hierarchy. Moreover, other administrative issues ranging from committee approval processes, differences in research and institutional culture, and intellectual property rights threaten the continuation and development of the partnership. As we trace the partnership's tremulous progress through the approval processes, particularly at the US campus, we can observe one example of how the shared codes of communication essential for global network membership are negotiated.

Because of the enormous weight and thus, wait, of academic processes at a large Land-grant institution, combined with the US dominance in accreditation and certification bodies, the Singapore institution adopts a number of US academic practices and models in order to meet the requirements of various administrative bodies at the US campus. Furthermore, the Singaporean government and institution intentionally strive to adopt US models in a number of key circumstances. While at first glance we might suppose that the dominant US institution is harrying the weaker Singaporean institution to follow its directives, a closer examination reveals that the Singapore government and university are exercising agency within this process, carefully choosing not only what policy to adopt but when to adopt them. As we will see, strategic appropriation of foreign practice is not unique to this case, but instead is in line with policies that the Singapore government and institutions have used since independence.

Moreover, it is not only the Singaporean campus that alters policy and procedure through the negotiations. The US campus also capitulates, though gradually, to the collaborative partnership model. Of course this is not necessarily an adherence to the network model in general, but may also be viewed as a variation of a competitive strategy. Nevertheless, it is a new form of competitive strategy in line with emerging models of international programming developing in the global knowledge economy.

Ultimately, this research allows us to view one example of the process that occurs as institutions negotiate the shared codes of communication that are necessary for the viability of the global network of higher education. In this case, much, though certainly not all, of that code is US in origin, yet we can see that the power in the relationship flows from both partner institutions in uneven and unpredictable ways.

Mediating Organizational Structures and Processes

Though key administrators and participating faculty from both institutions were in agreement about the goals of the program and even about the timeline and working details, documents from committees on the US campus paint a muddier picture for other administrators and faculty, particularly those serving on key campus committees.

The first obvious point of contention was the name of the program. While Singaporean documents continue to refer to a "joint PhD program," the US institution refers to the same program as "multi-institutional." When asked about the differing terminology, the Director for International Partnerships in the US explained that "joint degrees" refer to degrees between departments on campus, a joint degree between law and environmental biology, for example. When questioned why they referred to this degree as "multi" when it was only between two institutions, the Director explained that they were not expecting to add other institutions into this particular partnership, but they were establishing a model that might be used later. In future configurations, it might be possible to operate a similar collaboration between a number of institutions, though he stressed that no such programs were imminent (personal communication, March 12, 2009).

When asked why they didn't use the term "multi-institutional," staff members in the Singaporean international programs office explained that since Singapore had other joint degree programs, changing the name of this program would be confusing (personal communication, February 24, 26, 2009). This refusal to relent to terminology changes reveals both institutions holding firm to their own goals without acquiescing to the partner institution. Any resulting confusion for students seemed not to be a major concern for the administration at either institution.

Beyond differences in the name, the commencement of the program is another point of discrepancy between the institutions. For example, the Singaporean university was advertising a joint master's degree with the US institution by 2000 and a joint PhD as early as 2004. However, the proposal from the Midwestern Department of Chemical Engineering put before the faculty Senate September 6, 2001, requests only a "Study abroad Option in the Master of Science in Chemical Engineering." When the sponsoring faculty member was asked about this discrepancy, he explained that through the negotiations in the College committees and in the Graduate College, concessions had been made. "It became clear after endless rounds of meetings that we needed to start slower, to slow it down and take it step by step through this process." He goes on to explain that "without meaning to, we had stepped on some toes. We hadn't gone through all the proper steps to let everyone, and by that I mean at the college level, the Grad. college level, to see what we were doing. They hadn't had time to get on board" (personal communication, February 19, 2009).

Indeed, tracing the program through the committee minutes on the US campus, it is clear that a great deal of time was necessary to bring various necessary units of governance "on board." Unlike the Singapore campus, in order to gain approval at the US campus, the program needed to pass the Department of Chemical Engineering, the College of Engineering, the Graduate College, and the Faculty Senate, followed by the Board of Trustees, and finally the state governing board.

Tracking the progression through the Faculty Senate provides a more detailed timeline for the approval process. For example, the "Study Abroad Option" is approved for the MS in Chemical Engineering in October of 2001. It is not until September 2003 that we see the approval of the "Joint Program" option for the PhD in Chemical Engineering. Then, it is not until February 2006 that the proposal to generate guidelines for the development of a multi-institutional degree is put forward, but moved to "pending" as it is determined that more information is needed. By August 2006, the issue was referred to a subcommittee for review. A second subcommittee was convened to review the proposed guidelines developed by the first subcommittee on April 16, 2007. On October 1, 2007, the Report of the Task Force was sent to the Graduate College Executive Committee and the College of Liberal Arts and Sciences. On October 22, 2007, the Senate Committee on Educational Policy approved the proposal and forwarded it to the faculty senate. The senate approved the proposed guidelines on November 5, 2007. The specific multi-institutional agreement between the two institutions was not approved by the Senate until November 2008.

Once approved in the Senate, it moved on to the Board of Trustees (BOT). At the first submission of the Multi-institutional Proposal, the BOT sent it back with a request for further information. Then, by March 11 of 2009, more than ten years after the partner institutions had first collaborated on degree programs, the BOT approved the proposal and sent it forward to the state governing board for final approval. The program was approved;

however, the guidelines for multi-institutional degrees were not approved, suggesting that the BOT will view each program on a case-by-case basis in the future, rather than evaluating programs for meeting pre-established guidelines. This particular decision was a source of frustration for the chair of the committee that had worked to establish the guidelines. "We worked very carefully, and followed best practices from other institutions. I couldn't imagine why they weren't approved" (personal communication, April 23, 2009). The chair of the Education Policy Committee was less affected claiming that "we can rely on them ourselves. They were not meant to be laws, but just guidelines for use" (personal communication, April 28, 2009).

Examining only the document trail of the program as it plodded through committees, it appears as if there were long periods of time with inaction or inattention. In fact, interviews with key participants suggest that a great deal of administrative effort was being expended by both campuses in order to move the program approval forward. By closely following this process of negotiation, we can trace how some elements of the program get solidified into policy at both campuses, while other elements are sloughed away. This is significant since due to the regional and growing global importance of the involved institutions, we can assume that the ratified policy and program model become part of the shared code of operation of the global network of higher education.

Equivalency through Evaluation and Accreditation

As noted in the previous chapter, when the partnership was first initiated, the participant institutions did not behave as equal partners. However, in the context of the enormous growth occurring at the Singapore university, particularly in the Chemical Engineering department and related industries in Singapore, the institution was eager to establish its new position in the global hierarchy of higher education. In an effort to be known as "world class," comprehensive reviews of undergraduate and postgraduate curricula were conducted in the late 1990s (Mok, 2008). In addition, an international team of 11 prominent academics from top American, European, and Asian universities was invited to conduct a comprehensive review. The team made a number of recommendations, including broadening the curricula, integrating disciplines, drawing closer links between the universities and industry as well as continued expansion of postgraduate studies (Mok, 2008). In addition to these reviews, the department of Chemical Engineering invited the Accreditation Board for Engineering and Technology (ABET) to conduct an evaluation using substantial equivalency procedures used for parallel accreditation of US engineering programs. The findings statement to the institution states that the program in Chemical Engineering is "judged to meet the general and program specific ABET requirements for programs of that type," with ten pages of comments and suggestions.

Each of these evaluations is based on expertise coming from outside Singapore, and in the case of the ABET evaluation, is "primarily based upon the US system of engineering education and practice." While we cannot determine it absolutely, there is no evidence in documents or interviews to suggest that the US institution asked Singapore to submit to any such evaluations, though certainly adherence to standards of practice would have been well received by faculty and administration on the US campus who were working for the program acceptance. These aspirations follow Bourdieu's analysis, what he calls the legitimation and cultural capital acquired through accreditation. The impetus for the reviews and evaluations seems to come primarily from the Singaporean government and from within the Singaporean department itself as noted in their policy directives outlined by the Singaporean government. As we will continue to see, this appropriation of foreign models is a pattern that the Singapore government and institutions have consistently used to spur development.

Brand management.

According to an Associate Dean in Student Services who served on the Educational Policy committee at Midwestern university and who chaired the sub-committee in charge of developing guidelines for multi-institutional degrees, "the biggest hurdle was brand. No one wanted to do anything that would impact the brand of the institution" (personal communication, April 22, 2009). She went on to describe other international activities that in her opinion, actually had greater potential to damage the image of the institution, and yet were subject to far less scrutiny than the multi-institutional degree program. "The difference is, when you put another name on the diploma, you are suggesting that the other institution is somehow equal. This is something that makes [Midwestern university] very uncomfortable. After all, we see ourselves in competition with other institutions" (personal communication, April 22, 2009). Though not directly spoken in the US university committee documents, it seems clear from corroborating interviews of participants that the equal partnership was precisely the point of contention for some administrators and faculty. "Admitting we are equal to another institution, particularly one in some obscure sounding place like Singapore, is something we are loathe to do" the Associate Dean explained, smiling and shaking her head (personal communication, April 22, 2009). This competitive emphasis on "Brand" clearly follows the market driven model of international programming. Rather than moving to adopt an emerging model based on global networks in the global economy, some faculty and administrators continue to evaluate this program along market driven criteria including the view that other institutions are the "competition" rather than potentially equal partners.

Indeed, a number of other participants also felt that perceptions about the need to protect Midwestern's brand were a primary barrier. The Chair of the Education Policy Committee remarked that it was the committee's charge to "protect the University brand". (personal communication, April 28, 2009). A faculty member in Chemical Engineering explained that "we did not want to link up our name with [Singapore university's name] unless we were sure that they were of equal standing. In some ways, they [Singapore university] could well be our equal, maybe superior at some point, but it is reputation, well, the brand, that we had to be thinking about" (personal communication, June 11, 2009).

Similarly, the former Head of the Department claimed that one of the main risks in any new program is what he termed "the red faced test." He explained that "no one wants to end up in the papers with a red face" (personal communication, February 24, 2009). He blamed this "fear of embarrassment" for the "brand of the institution" for the slow approval process at Midwestern university (personal communication, February 24, 2009).

The above participants' responses seem to suggest that some administrators and faculty at the US institution were viewing the relationships between institutions in competitive terms, operating from market-like imperatives. Indeed, the repeated use of the term "brand" in reference to an institution reflects what some have called mission creep (Knight, 2003) and the commericialization or marketization of higher education (Slaughter & Leslie, 1997; Marginson, 1995; Considine et al., 2001). According to interviews, proponents of the program continued to be frustrated by what they viewed as some administrators' inability to move beyond or outside of this competition based framework and instead begin to see this partnership as a cooperative venture.

Differences in Research and Institutional Culture

Issues of equivalency and "brand" were only a few of many barriers that the new model of degree program faced. As we might expect, various cultural differences impacted the program planning as well. From school year calendar, to the differences between the US system and Singapore's British based system, all of the numerous details typical of international program planning had to be negotiated. In addition, because this program was a research based partnership, further matters surrounding the institutional and national cultures of research, and even science, had to be resolved.

Research cultural differences.

In this increasingly global age of science, and with the dominance of US higher education models worldwide, we might expect a seamless transition between functions of chemical engineering departments more or less anywhere in the world. However, there were perceived differences in the research culture. According to faculty at both institutions, US research culture places more responsibility on the student than is typically the case in Singapore. PhD students in the US are often expected to conceive of their own research projects and then argue for their importance. In contrast, Singaporean faculty are more directive, informing students of the research agenda and where students should try to fit into it. Singaporean students get used to being directed and behave accordingly.

According to a faculty member from Chemical Engineering at the US institution, "Singaporean students often operate with the idea that the answer is known in the back of some book somewhere, and their job is just to have to find it" (personal communication, April 22, 2009). According to the current Department Head, "Singapore trains hard working test takers, but debating with the advisor, letting the creativity fly, that's not their strength" (personal communication, February 19, 2009). However, both faculty and administrators confirmed that, "after an initial period of tentativeness, most will thrive, while only a few don't" (personal communication, February 19, 2009).

Evidence from policy documents reveals that the difference in research style was one of the driving forces for the Singaporean side of the partnership. In fact, Midwestern university's expectation of creative, critical thinking students corresponded precisely with the Singaporean government's 1997 policy initiative, "Thinking Schools, Learning Nation" (TSLN). As noted in chapter three, the new Singaporean curriculum intervention included an emphasis on the teaching of critical thinking and of developing creativity in students. Adopting the US style of creative, student driven research seems to be an underlying goal of the program. However, as noted, some critics doubt the efficacy of teaching about or learning critical thinking and creativity in a hierarchical education structure that favors exams (Lee, 2008; Koh, 2004). Others argue that "creativity will not blossom to its fullest when governmentality is normalized [as it is argued to be] in the Singaporean habitus" (Koh, 2004).

However, if we look back to other policy initiatives of the Singaporean government, we can see that transplanted modes implemented through top down initiatives have been adopted comprehensively in the past. For example, after notable divisions in social mobility and class between the English-educated and the non-English educated and the resulting widespread unrest, the Singaporean government determined that English was to be the medium of instruction in all schools, and the other three official mother tongues, Chinese, Malay, and Tamil, were to be taught as second languages. The government argued successfully for English because of its use in the world of business, science and technology (Hill & Lian, 1995). We might guess that an educational emphasis on critical thinking and creativity could be appropriated with less potential for resistance than appropriating the "native tongue of the colonial master [to be] indigenized as a national language of Singapore" (Koh, 2009; p. 337). Regardless of the debates surrounding the potential for success of government mandated creativity, it is clear that adopting or imitating from a foreign source is a strategy employed by the Singaporean government.

Stepping towards the Joint PhD

Despite these government policies and the extensive evaluations and reviews, faculty in Chemical Engineering at Midwestern still needed to be convinced of the research skills of Singaporean students, particularly their ability to survive in a US research degree program.

The current Department Head of Chemical Engineering was a faculty member when the initial master's program was first developed. He explained that from the start, to his understanding, the goal of establishing the master's degree was to build engagement between the two institutions before moving on to develop the PhD program. "[The former Department Head] was very smart. He realized he needed to build engagement before we went to full blown doctoral program" (personal communication, February 19, 2009).

He explained that the master's program was a departure for the department. "Look, we do research. We haven't run terminal master's degrees. What we do tends to feed into PhD programs — research. The master's degree was created consciously as a stepping stone [to the PhD]. We hoped to continue the program, but when the funding fell apart, we had to let it go. But we still held on to the original idea of the PhD" (personal communication, February 19, 2009).

When asked how the program planners hoped to move forward when the "stepping stone" fell apart, he responded that the goal of the stepping stone had been met. That is, the two departments from the partner institutions had forged a bond, a working relationship, and were collaborating on research in some key areas. "Our faculty were always more interested in research, and so a PhD program is in some ways easier to wrap our heads around" (personal communication, February 19, 2009). But it wasn't an automatic next step. "What was missing was any evidence that students from Singapore could handle the research. We knew they were good, but could they do the research component?" (personal communication, February 19, 2009).

At about the same time that the master's degree was beginning to show cracks in financial viability, a chemical engineering faculty member at Midwestern brought in a Singapore student through other research connections, and that student did very well. "It was just one student, but it was our existence proof. We decided, now we can talk about PhD" (personal communication, February 19, 2009). The Department Head estimates that it was around 2000 when the chemical engineering department began to seriously pursue the multi-institutional PhD. The MOU was not signed until 2004. He explained that for a program to be viable, they had to be able to show to faculty and to campus committees that Singaporean students would thrive in the American research university environment.

Institutional cultural differences.

Significant cultural differences were reported between the institutions as well. First, despite the fact that many of the faculty members at the Singapore institution had been educated in the US, the shared governance model of the US institution at times became a source of frustration for faculty and administrators accustomed to the more nimble model at the Singaporean institution. According to a faculty member in Chemical Engineering at the Singaporean university,

> we felt very reassured when administrators and faculty were here, and we would talk things over, but it often seemed that some of what was happening on the home campus was beyond their control. Even though the faculty in the department and top administrators at the university wanted the degree program, they could not be assured of program approval. This is a different situation to us. (personal communication, February 26, 2009)

Because of the shared governance model, quick decisions are less likely at a large US institution, as faculty and administrators from across campus have to understand and then approve the program. In Singapore, decisions follow a top down model, making program approval much more expedient.

For their part, administrators and faculty at the US institution reported being discomposed or flummoxed by the Singapore university's strict adherence to key performance indicators, or KPIs. As the current department chair explained, "this shows up in measurements of everything, how many papers published, the impact factor, everything in quantitative measures, rule bound, one size fits all" (personal communication, February 19, 2009). KPIs seemed to be a source of anxiety as well. "The biggest risk is not meeting them. That's how programs close," the Campus Legal Counsel explained. When asked if Midwestern would be able to meet the KPIs set for this program, he shook his head and shrugged.

> It depends. There are only so many qualified applicants, and in order to be qualified, those students will be very high level, with lots of other options. We have to hope they choose this program. That's why funding is so important – without it, we can't compete. Funding is essential to attract students from a tight pool of qualified Singapore students. Success comes down to KPIs. (personal communication, March 18, 2009)

In both interviews and in documents, it becomes apparent that KPIs are the Singaporean way of asserting its own requirements into the global flows of power. Indeed, it is through KPIs that Singapore is able to wield its own means of a culturally mediated structure of power as outlined previously (Bourdieu, 1996). Due to the numerical nature of the KPIs, they can begin to appear as a "perfectly neutral authority" (Bourdieu, 1996) thereby camouflaging the power structure. Since power is symbolically produced and maintained by cultural models, the university can occupy a central, critical position. KPIs force the partner institution, US in this case, to submit to Singapore's standard measure, revealing a realignment or shift in power relations between the two partner institutions. In the US institution's deference to meet or attempt to meet the KPIs, the repositioning of the Singapore institution becomes evident. The Singapore university is no longer a "lesser" institution following a colonial model, but a partner capable of initiating its own requirements for the collaboration. Documents reveal that KPIs are the means by which programs are forced to cease operation in Singapore (see Strait Times regarding Johns Hopkins). Moreover they are used to direct the collaboration in particular ways.

In addition to adjusting to the new measure of KPIs, the level of detail orientation with regard to funding was a point of adjustment for US faculty, too. "This shows up in reimbursements, other day to day business operations" (personal communication, April 22, 2009). As one Assistant Dean at Midwestern university explained, "US faculty are entrepreneurial and less detail focused. The institution tries to support faculty. At [Singapore institution], faculty bend to the needs of the institution" (personal communication, April 22, 2009). Faculty at Midwestern also reported differences in level of responsibility assumed for funding. "The biggest difference is that [Singapore] faculty don't write grants. The administrative structure is large and comfortable, so [faculty] are not worried about paying bills" (personal communication, March 13, 2009). Faculty on the US campus, in contrast, operate in a system that heavily emphasizes funding acquisitions in the form of grants, particularly at a research institution and in the sciences.

Finally, faculty members on both sides of the partnership mentioned the differences in perceptions that occur due to geographic location. Singapore professors mentioned the need to attract the best students from the region due to Singapore's aging population and small size. A professor on the US side explained that "Singapore gets globalization in a distilled form you don't see anywhere else. They are very conscious of their place in the globe. Here in the US, the US is so big, the rest of world is less important" (personal communication, March 13, 2009). An Associate Dean in Student Services on the US campus explained that "it is hard for us to see why we need this kind of arrangement. For them, a small city state, partnerships are more obvious. We are just busy competing with the Big Ten and others around the Midwest" (personal communication, April 22, 2009). In this perception of globalization, the Singaporean institution leads the US as it perceives the global value of collaboration, while the US institution continues to see others from a competitive standpoint.

Negotiating Intellectual Property

While the debates dragged on in the Midwestern campus committees and the Singapore institution continued to extend and vet its programs, legal counsel from both campuses struggled to sort through the tangled web of intellectual property issues. According to the Director for International Partnerships at Midwestern, negotiations surrounding intellectual property (IP) rights presented the biggest challenge to the partnership. "That part took the longest of all to negotiate," he explained (personal communication, March 12, 2009). As described in chapter three, since the Bayh-Dole Act of 1980, universities retain the rights of intellectual property developed by their faculty. Under this partnership, those rights would need to be shared as well as protected.

Campus Legal Counsel for Midwestern university explained that much of the work was trailblazing, as it was beyond the scope of typical arrangements. While the university retains a staff that works to protect faculty development and licensing, this project would depart from typical licensing in two key ways. First, the joint ownership that this partnership necessitated is "completely different from our usual work in IP" (personal communication, March 18, 2009), requiring joint ownership and potentially joint licensing. Second, protecting IP rights internationally would be more challenging than protecting IP domestically. According to the Deputy Legal Counsel at Midwestern, though the university had some experience with these matters, "it is very complex and expensive if you want to protect IP rights worldwide" (personal communication, March 18, 2009). Nevertheless, Midwestern's Legal Counsel explained that the extended efforts were important enough to pursue. "It was obvious that this program would lead to research opportunities and funding for projects that we wouldn't have otherwise been able to do" (personal communication, March 18, 2009). In addition to the complexity inherent in the US shared governance system requiring transparency and complex decentralized reporting, certain obligations were embedded in Singapore law, including issues of opening bank accounts, hiring auditors, all of which had to be considered in negotiations and operations (personal communication, March 18, 2009).

To appreciate that complexity, we must place the program development within the historical context of IP law in Singapore. As noted in chapter three, by 1985, the US-based International Intellectual Property Alliance report declared that "Singpaore is truly the world capital of piracy" (Uphoff, 1991, p.13). At that time, copyright piracy was "a more or less acceptable occupation, and pirates were estimated to control 80-90% of the tape-market" (Uphoff, 1991, p. 13). The operations were so extensive that an estimated $270 million worth of pirated tapes and books were shipped throughout Asia from Singapore in 1984 making Singapore a piracy hub of Asia (Uphoff, 1991). Due to the large amount of popular cultural products from the US, American companies began pressuring the Singaporean government to enforce and reform copyright laws. Despite pressure from the US and the international community, the Singaporean government argued that it would change its laws when it was in Singapore's interest to do so (Ramcharan, 2006, p. 323).

In Singapore's typically nimble fashion, policies were reversed to the extent that by 2002, Singapore was rated the most "IP protective" country in Asia by the Political & Economic Risk Consultancy (qtd in Ramcharan, 2006, p. 322). This dramatic, rapid and stringent adoption of IP protection occurred for several reasons. First, IP was included as point of discussion during the Uruguay Round of the GATT (Knight, 2003). Without accepting IP protection, Singapore would be severely compromised in trade negotiations. Second, pressure from the US increased as knowledge intensive goods began to occupy a larger share of US exports (Uphoff, 1991). Finally, Singapore faced the threat of loss of benefits under the General System of Preferences. After largely symbolic hearings of a Parliamentary Select Committee and consultations with US delegates, the Copyright Act was passed in early 1987. The shift to a knowledge based economy has spurred the continued enforcement of copyright as a part of the strategic plan. Indeed, copyright industries in Singapore now constitute a significant amount of the national wealth (Ramcharan, 2006, 332). Here again we see Singapore strategically "copying everything" in order to build its economy. The protection of IP is another example of Singapore adopting, even embracing, a foreign transplantation for its own advancement.

Despite earlier protestations that IP would keep Singapore on the periphery, it is now generally held to be one of the nation's key tenets as a global knowledge hub (Lee, 2008; Ramcharan, 2006). Indeed, administrators and legal counsel at Midwestern site IP protection chief among many when enumerating Singapore's appealing attributes.

> One of the most attractive features of Singapore is the respect for IP law. Of course it is a safe place, a gateway, but in comparison to say, China, or India, places with burgeoning education markets and needs, Singapore has the respect for rule of law which makes it a better place to engage in research. (Director for International Partnerships at Midwestern, personal communication, March 12, 2009)

The Campus Counselor for the Midwestern university similarly stated that "despite the numerous differences in our legal systems, because Singapore protects IP, we at least had a starting point" (personal communication, March 18, 2009). This narrative reveals not only the importance of IP, but the distinct characteristics of a research based partnership. Moving beyond "markets and needs," the criteria of international programming in previous development models, this emerging model has differing criteria that includes protection of IP in order for the program to function. Because of the importance of managing research output in products or spin off products, IP becomes an important component. The shadow of the market is traceable in this new cooperative model in this manner, as related products serve as an important point of negotiation.

Though legal counsel from both partner institutions were reluctant to give specific details of the negotiations or to share documents detailing the specific agreement, both sides stated that they were pleased with the resulting terms and felt it benefited each individual institution as well as the partnership as a whole. Midwestern's Deputy Legal Counsel explained that

> Singapore gets first rights to develop any product that comes from the research, but we get second rights. Beyond that, we also get half of what they develop. It's perfect for us since that kind of commercialization in Asia is certainly not our primary goal of this program. (personal communication, March 18, 2009)

He went on to say that "they would be better at that anyway. We are happy to get half of whatever comes from it" (personal communication, March 18, 2009).

When asked if Midwestern university had "copied" any other models or followed any other institutions, the US Legal Counsel said they had looked to other models from other institutions. He commented that there were two other institutions that were consulted, and more recently, another institution had sought advice from Midwestern university staff (personal communication, March 18, 2009). Clearly, in this case, IP protection has been cemented as a necessary component of the shared codes of operation necessary for higher education network membership.

Approval of the Multi-institutional Degree

The state board of higher education approved the multi-institutional degree program in spring of 2009. Despite the long process and numerous cliffhangers along the way, when participants at the US institution were asked if the process could have been more expedient, all of them said no. Members of the Education Policy committee explained that "we needed to spend time with such an important proposal," and "we worked carefully, which is not a quick process" (personal communication, June 11, 2009). The chair of the committee went further saying, "this should never be an immediate endorsement. A world class institution will not just join into a partnership without a significant history between the two institutions" (personal communication, April 28, 2009). The Department Head echoed this sentiment saying that "I might wish it could all happen quickly, but in the end, the institution needs to take time to be sure that it is making the right move" (personal communication, February 19, 2009). The Director of International Research admitted that some momentum had been lost due to the long process, but felt that with the official approval, the faculty and students would reengage and become energized about the program again. "Now that it is in place, we can stir up interest," he explained (personal communication, March 12, 2009).

In Singapore, the reaction to the process was far less positive. According to an outside examiner of the program for Singapore university, "the pace was very slow. It was disappointing to faculty, to the students, when the approvals did not come quickly" (personal communication, February 25, 2009). A faculty member remembers frustration when "it kept being sent to this committee, and then another committee. We had a signed MOU, so we didn't see why it was so slow" (personal communication, February 24, 2009). Another faculty member explained that "we had hoped to grow the program and develop it right away, but it always kept getting pushed back. We started working with other institutions just to go forward" (personal communication, February 26, 2009). Another faculty member remarked that "it was new for us when it started, but because of that, it seemed to take a long time. We liked the people we were working with at [Midwestern], but in the meantime, we began developing programs elsewhere that went more smoothly" (personal communication, February 25, 2009). The former Department chair was more careful, saying only that "we wanted it to go quickly, but it seemed that something happened. I don't know, but it did take some time to be approved" (personal communication, February 25, 2009).

Perhaps the most vocal was the former Department chair from the US, now on staff at a major government funded research agency in Singapore.

> We just could not keep it going. Time after time we'd get it to [various] committee[s] and there would be this concern or that one. We were there trying to drag the institution forward and all the while it is pulling back, resisting. It's tragic really because the momentum was lost. All the original people who cared so much in the beginning don't care anymore. They have moved on. The programs have moved on. The institution has moved on. (personal communication, February 24, 2009)

When pressed further and asked if it even mattered now if the program were approved, he shrugged and said, "the benefit will come somewhere else. Some other program will come along and benefit from all the work we did, but it won't be this program, and it won't be in Chemical Engineering in Singapore" (personal communication, February 24, 2009).

The one outlying voice in Singapore came from the former Dean of Engineering at Midwestern university, the one who had envisioned the program so many years before on the boat speeding through the Singapore harbor. Now, like the former department chair that used to work for him at Midwestern, he lives and works in Singapore. After a number of years as Dean at Midwestern, he had been hired by the President of Singapore university to "Americanize the place and make it a world class institution" (personal communication, February 25, 2009). Three presidents later, he is still advisor to the President at Singapore university.

I expected that he would be frustrated that his original idea had taken so long to come to fruition. Instead, after a pause he said, "the process should not be evaluated for speed. There is no non-destructive test on a student's education. We must, therefore, be very careful. . ." (personal communication, February 25, 2009).

The Existence Proof

To understand the significance of the new program model, we can begin by examining the interpretations of what participants have called "the existence proof," that is, the multi-institutional degree in its newly approved status on the US campus and its status in Singapore as one of a number of joint degree programs. Though the two institutions are now formally linked in the issuance of the PhD degree, some of their perceptions of its current status cast them apart, disjointed in their assessment of the program's potentials. The approved form of the program illuminates a few final aspects of the planning process. The final form of the approved multi-institutional degree at the Midwestern and Singapore universities contained a number of elements of interest to this study.

First, both institutions will be equally represented on the diploma or seal that students receive at the end of the program. As we have seen in this chapter, this represents a compromise on the part of some administrators and faculty at the US institution and seems to symbolize a tacit acceptance of the Singaporean institution as a comparable if not equal partner. While we cannot assume that the US institution is necessarily moving into a non-competitive mode of international collaboration beyond market strategies, we can find that this type of collaboration represents at the very least a new kind of competitive strategy, one that recognizes the importance of global network membership and global partnerships. Moreover, this global partner is not viewed as a recipient of aid, or strictly as a market, but is being acknowledged as a worthy collaborator evidenced in the shared seal on the diploma of the program.

For Singapore, this symbolizes the institution's ascendancy beyond the colonial patterns of some past international programming to the status of a full participating member in an international partnership with a world class institution. While other such arrangements have been made with other institutions, this was the first institution with which Singapore university began such a process and co-envisioned the shared degree, so to share the graduating scroll with this particular institution held symbolic importance for those who had worked on the program from the beginning. According to a faculty member at Singapore university, "we spent a lot of time designing it, getting the look of the scroll just right. It shows that both [institutions] played an equal role. That means something to us, and of course to our students" (personal communication, February 26, 2009).

A second notable feature of the approved program is that the Singapore government sponsored funding agency is, at the time of this research, providing funding only for students from Singapore. Administrators at the US campus lamented that US companies or other entities would not sponsor US students for the program. The Department Chair of Chemical Engineering at Midwestern stressed that the program is set up so that US students could participate. That is, there are no curricular or structural barriers to US participants. Regarding the funding, he was "optimistic" that funding would be located so that US students would eventually be able to be a part of the program too. However, the Director of International Research Partnerships was less optimistic of the immediate prospects of funding for US students, explaining that US companies are reluctant to fund PhD programs because such programs take a long time to complete, and the research results can take a long time to materialize into marketable products or useable materials (personal communication, March 12, 2009).

Despite the current lack of resources for US students to participate in the program, administrators and faculty were quick to point to other benefits of the approved program for Midwestern. First, the Department Chair in Chemical Engineering explained that the multi-institutional degree program will be used as a recruiting tool to show the global reach of the campus, and specifically the department (personal communication, February 19, 2009). Here again, following his predecessor, is the reiteration of the importance of global network membership as explained in earlier chapters. Further, the department chair also made clear that students benefit from faculty engagement abroad, because it develops a global perspective in faculty which can then be expressed and developed in the classroom and in research (personal communication, February 19, 2009). Next, he explained that support in Singapore allows funding for projects that the National Institutes of Health might not fund. Echoing the relationship between engineering education and national funding sources, he stated that national funding is limited to certain topics and is subject to lengthy approval processes. This international program provides funding to pursue ideas without that lengthy approval process (personal communication, February 19, 2009). Moreover, through the connection to the petrol-chemical hub in Singapore, the departments' research portfolio will be more diverse. This is an important status since "the federal government only funds certain projects, yet multi-nationals want students to have other skills, so this is making students employable" (personal communication, February 19, 2009).

The Director of International Research Partnerships also stressed the value of the multi-institutional degree program in terms of National Science Foundation funding. He explained that the NSF encourages most proposals to require an international component (personal communication, March 12, 2009). Having the connection to international partners, particularly partners that broaden the capacity through facilities, increases the competitiveness of national funding proposals (personal communication, March 12, 2009). Clearly the triple helix is being complicated by the introduction of outside funding sources through these emerging programs in the global higher education network.

Another point of consideration for the approved PhD program is what it meant for the institutions moving forward. After the program was approved on the US campus, several administrators and faculty were asked about the significance of that approval with regard to the planning process of future programs or future policy changes. Now that one program had set the groundwork, serving as "the existence proof," perhaps future similar programs would be adopted more quickly, or be subject to a different type or length of review. The Chair of the Education Policy Committee explained that

> no other program is imminent. We are not opposed to other programs, but at the same time, everything has to be in place. That all takes time. There is no reason to think that future programs would move through the approval process quickly. (personal communication, April 28, 2009)

The Department Chair of Chemical Engineering agreed, explaining that "You have to have the right caliber institution, a funding model that works, students that want to do this, faculty have to see their own interest met. It all must be very compelling" (personal communication, February 19, 2009). He explained that no other program was immediately in line to be approved. Citing several partnerships that the department is involved in currently, the Department Chair further explained that

> a multi-institutional degree is not something you start with, you have to spend a number of years, and other programs can't get out of the gate without the time and engagement, and a huge capital investment that this program had from the beginning. Campus must be open to this, with administrators willing to fertilize at key points, travel money, support, and pushing proposals through. (personal communication, February 19, 2009)

The Director for International Research Partnerships agreed that future programs would be subject to the same level of review as this first multi-institutional degree, but believed that the process would run more smoothly now that this program was in place (personal communication, March 12, 2009). A faculty member who had served on committees to develop the program agreed, explaining that, "before, faculty and administrators were being asked to envision something that did not previously exist. Now, we can look to, or point to, this example" (personal communication, April 22, 2009).

The Director of the International Programs office at the US institution was also optimistic about the future of additional multi-institutional degree programs at Midwestern. "Because this program was for a Professional degree, which will increasingly require a global component, I see a bright future for multi-institutional degrees." He went on to caution that "One obstacle is if students see it as a disincentive to spend more time towards graduation, then you will have difficulty getting US students involved" (personal communication, April 7, 2009). He stressed the need to continually think of how to bring institutions together in such a way that students are not forced into a longer commitment in time to complete the degree for graduation. Engineering in particular is a program that already can take from four and a half to five years to complete. Moreover, he stressed that "quality assurance work is essential. [The program should] start small, and grow out of a curricular need. Embellishing, growing a relationship, takes a steady commitment from the same faculty over time. That is hard to sustain" (personal communication, April 7, 2009).

For the Singapore side of the partnership, the implications for the final approval seemed more limited to the impact on the students who would be participating, as well as anticipated results from their research (personal communication, February 25, 2009). Moreover, participants spoke of the impact those students would make on future students, describing the circular benefits of education for the continued development of Singapore as a regional knowledge hub (personal communication, February 26, 2009). Participants pointed out that other international joint degrees had been established before this one achieved final approval, making it one of several instead of the first one (personal communication, February 26, 2009). While participants on the Singapore campus were pleased to know of its final approval in the US, the primary goals they had originally established for the degree were now being shared by a number of similar types of programs.

Finally, from the beginning of the planning process for this program to its final approved form, personal relationships play an essential role. In fact, the personal relationships that develop from the beginning of the program continue throughout the planning process. Without the trust and respect developed over face-to-face meetings, as well as through years of correspondence, the program would likely not have come to final authorization. According to faculty and administrators at both institutions, it was the face-to-face contact that actually allowed the departments to begin to form collaborations. This is contrary to the emphasis often placed on the electronic communication's indispensable role in the network society. Certainly, such quick communication was essential for maintaining relationships, but most all participants spoke of face-to-face interactions as the most important factor driving and sustaining the partnership. To illustrate, in a final follow up interview with the Director for International Research Partnerships, he opened an email and photo he had just received from the son of the former Director of the EDB in Singapore, the son who had attended Midwestern university a number of years ago at the beginning of the program planning process. The photo showed the young man and his child standing in his research lab at another world-class US university where the son had recently received tenure. The US administrator's pleasure and pride at the photo were evident (personal communication, March 12, 2009). Clearly, the personal networks are as important in this case as the electronic connections that facilitate them.

Conclusion

Because of Singapore's colonial past, it is tempting to view the process of program development with a US university through a post-colonial lens, viewing the relationship as forming from the powerful center of US higher education dominating and directing the terms to what we might call the periphery in Singapore. However, interviews and documents reveal that in this case, the negotiations are informed by isomorphism developing more from appropriation rather than direct imposition.

Turning to the global network of higher education, both institutions have chosen to extend beyond historical patterns. The US institution redefined the terms of its historical contract traditionally held with its locally rooted constituencies to include global network membership as a priority for the institution and stakeholders. Moreover, the US institution comes to accept the multi-institutional model, albeit slowly and carefully.

The Singaporean institution, too, reconfigured its place in the global hierarchy, rejecting colonial patterns of engagement and, instead, followed methods of strategic appropriation that it has used for advancement since Independence.

Conflicting organizational structures, cultural differences and intellectual property issues must be negotiated in order for the partnership to progress. As we know from Castells as well as Appadurai, network membership requires shared codes of communication (2009). Tracing the negotiation of these communication codes in this case reveals the complexity that informs the global isomorphism in higher education. As this study illuminates, adopting the ways of the other can actually be a means of seizing power, rather than of succumbing to it. The Singaporean government uses appropriation to garner and develop its own economic strength. Moreover, in contrast to what neoliberal narratives might expect, we find the former colonial peripheral government and, by extension, institution in Singapore able to resist supranational forces such as the WTO to choose, perhaps not "if," but "when" to implement its legally binding policy directives. Further, Singapore is also able to assert its own requirements into the collaboration through the reliance on KPIs.

Though many of the resulting shared codes of communication appear to be US in origin, the isomorphism results not solely from hegemonic chauvinism, but from strategic adoption of proven methods aimed at economic advancement through educational policy. Moreover, it is likely that the imitations and negotiations found in this case will replicate further due to the position of each institution as a regional hub. Now that such patterns are in place and the codes have been established, further replication becomes even more likely, contributing to the isomorphism that we have seen around the globe.

Dominance of US higher education remains an undisputed fact (Altbach, 2004a; Knight, 2003; Green & Olson, 2003), but attributing global isomorphism to global flows from center to periphery proves overly simplistic in light of this case. This chapter has shown that the shared codes of operation for the global network of higher education are developed through negotiation, with push/pull factors emerging from local demands both subject to and in resistance against international forces. Further, those local demands originate at both sites of the study.

CHAPTER SEVEN

The Existence Proof

Introduction

This case study has examined the planning process of a multi-institutional degree program between a research institution in the US and in Singapore, a new model of collaboration in international higher education functioning within a global network. As an explorative study, this research does not lead to direct recommendations regarding this specific program or others like it, or suggest direct policy outcomes. Instead, this final chapter reviews the central themes uncovered by the study and considers their importance for current understanding and for future research.

Stepping back from the particularities, we can begin to understand this program as a part of a larger narrative. Representing just two nodes in the global network, this study sheds light on the actual functioning of the global network of higher education, capturing the particularities of history and culture that impact the flows of power amidst the power of flows.

Main Findings and Implications

Thematic summary.

Through evidence gathered in interviews and documents at both the US institution and at the Singaporean institution, rationales, barriers, and possibilities emerge in the planning process of an international multi-institutional degree.

US rationales.

First, global network membership was an apparent rationale for Midwestern for pursing and persevering through this program development. Not only did faculty and administrators want to provide a global experience for students, but they wanted to be "top of mind" in the global network of higher education. Olds has argued that for foreign institutions, a primary rationale for operating in Singapore is for universities to extend their own network into Singapore and the broader Asian network (2007). Given the emphasis on the research potential at Jurong Island as well as the emphasis on protecting IP rights for program planners and for administrators that approved the program, this rationale seems to have played a part in this program development since participants at the US institution so often characterized this connection to Singapore university in terms of the research collaborations such a partnership would enable. Moreover, according to the outside examiner of the program, the level of collaboration that the first incarnation of the program created for participating students went above and beyond what is typical in an international exchange program. Clearly, US program planners were strongly motivated to prepare students to work in collaborative global teams upon graduation. This reflects the trends in emerging models of international programming responding to global economic demands as noted in chapter three. Also, it reveals US program planners' perceptions of the importance of the global network operating in education and in an overlapping feedback loop with the network of global science. Because of the timing of the program development, it is possible to map this juncture as the point at which international programming moves into a new epoch, beyond the strict control of market-based models. Of course, the shadow of the market is still traceable in aspects of this program planning process, yet from the original conception to the actual fruition of approved program, it is clear that planners have changed their own perceptions and are recruiting new narratives as rationales of international engagement for their institutions.

Second, for the US institution, the rationales for pursuing the program are to some extent financial, as critics on that campus accused, but they are not *strictly* financial. Throughout the planning process, administrators were always also strongly motivated by the excellent quality of students, facilities, and research potential of the program in Singapore. It seems clear from interviews that without that multi-tiered excellence in the Singaporean education system, administrators and faculty on the US side would never have maintained the enthusiasms necessary to continually pursue the project despite a number of setbacks and delays along the way. Therefore, the pursuit of excellent students, excellent faculty collaborators, and excellent research facilities are rationales for Midwestern university.

It is fair to say, though, that excellence alone would also not have been sufficient to sustain the enthusiasms necessary to endure the long founding process. As noted, funding opportunities are also a rationale for program planners on the Midwestern campus. As Olds has stated, universities being courted by the Singaporean government and institutions were enticed through funding for everything from large research facilities to travel expenses (2007). For Midwestern, like other cash-strapped US universities that were experiencing continued state and federal cuts, the availability of funds is necessarily a rationale for program development. Moreover, the enormous costs associated with research intensive programs like chemical engineering make research facilities and funding opportunities enormously attractive. Even US national funding sources like NSF grants are increasingly tied to international collaboration. Therefore, such partnerships bring funding opportunities both through the original collaboration and in supporting additional opportunities through US government funding that are also tied to international engagement.

Finally, research opportunity is a clear rationale for the US institution, perhaps the principal rationale. Focused from the beginning on developing a PhD program, administrators and faculty at the department and campus level cite increased research opportunities for faculty and students as a primary rationale. Moreover, having a diverse research portfolio in the Chemical Engineering department is important for attracting and keeping faculty, for pursuing funding opportunities, as well as for recruiting students. As noted, the phenomenal growth occurring in Singapore in the petrol-chemical industry first encouraged administrators to establish the program. The newly adopted legal protection for IP rights further encouraged the pursuit of research developments that might lead to shared product development in Asia. Thus, the ideal environment for research created by the Singaporean government served as a strong rationale for the US institution.

Singapore's rationales.

With a stated goal of becoming a global knowledge hub, a primary rationale for the Singaporean institution and the government in developing this partnership was global education network membership. As Olds (2007), Mok (2008), Sidhu (2006) and others have shown, Singapore has developed its economy in part by developing the global competitiveness of its higher education system.

For the Singaporean institution then, a primary motivation throughout the program formation was development of its own capacity as a research institution and as a principal part of Singapore's global knowledge hub. As the Department Chair around the time of the program's first inception remembers, "we needed to be world class, and we needed to do it right then, without any hesitation or delay" (personal communication, February 25, 2009). With the enormous growth experienced in the region in knowledge intensive fields such as chemical processing on Jurong Island, the partnership with the US institution was a way to directly enhance capacity and to manage extraordinary growth. According to Richard Garrett, deputy director at the Observatory on Borderless Higher Education, the Singaporean government could not grow domestic capacity fast enough. Therefore, "transnational activity was viewed as a way to stem study abroad rates and to mentor local institutions, [yet] the long-term aim was greater self-sufficiency [for Singaporean institutions] (2003).

Specifically, the Singapore institution relied on the partnership as a way to learn and then model US practices viewed by the Singaporean government as the key to developing a creative, entrepreneurial citizenry. With a government aiming to be the "Boston of the East," the Singaporean university was under pressure to "Americanize" in a number of ways. As an example, the former Dean of Engineering from the US university was recruited by the President of the Singapore university to serve in an advising role and specifically to "Americanize the place."

As we have seen, adapting student expectations and behavior to the style of American higher education is yet another form of appropriation, a strategy that the Singapore government has used to spur economic development since independence. It is important to note that it was the Singaporean government that called for this adaptation, openly striving to make their top two universities the "Harvard and MIT of Asia". To that end, a series of comprehensive reviews were undertaken, first by the government and then by the universities themselves. In addition to becoming "world-class," a stated goal was to determine methods for students to become more creative (Mok, 2008, p. 165). From the 1997 strategic planning exercise forward, one of Singapore's universities clearly states "the mission of the university is to train people with enhanced capacity for innovation, creativity, and quality performance" (Mok, 2000, p. 166).

With policies like "Thinking Schools; Learning Nation" the rationales driving the Singaporean government's reliance on foreign institutions becomes more apparent. The concept of "thinking schools" entails education institutions developing future citizens capable of engaging in critical and creative thinking, while "learning nation" emphasizes that education is a life-long endeavor. Olds finds that "foreign institutions are recognized by the Singaporean state as playing a fundamental role in restructuring the economy" with the overall goal of aligning local universities in an entrepreneurial and business mindset following the US model, and to recruit increasing numbers of international students. According to Olds, "the logic behind this is to create networks that can be used in the enhancement of the research and teaching process" through the acquisition of research funding, industry feedback, and joint research (2007).

The Singaporean government continues to import expatriate workers and students, model top tier institutions and policies, and innovate in their higher education development, all strategies aimed at infusing creativity into the culture. For example, the National University of Singapore will soon open its first residential college in August of 2011. Again, following US models, University Town, as the dormitory is known, will house Professors, graduate and undergraduate students in a high-rise building designed to function as a platform for informal learning, with an emphasis on multidisciplinary issues. The university plans to foster "creative destruction," a disruption in which passive learning practices are destroyed and replaced with different perspectives on diverse topics (Purnell, 2010).

Despite the Singaporean government's spectacular success in terms of other economic and education initiatives, the question remains: can a creative citizenry be mandated? The answer will be important not just for Singapore itself, but for nations around the globe, who are increasingly pressured to innovate to compete in a knowledge based economy, an economic model that demands entrepreneurial, creative citizenry. Therefore, this study and the cultural milieu in which it is located become an important test case in which to observe the attempted importation and enforcement of innovation as a cultural form. The extent to which the Singaporean educational culture, and the culture at large, will be able to adapt is still unclear. Whether "creativity" can be copied like a music CD, or blends to a hybrid, a kind of Singlish, or is even resisted at the local level, remains to be seen.

Barriers impacting the US and Singapore partnership.

Beyond the obvious barriers of distance, time, and differences in education system, this study has uncovered some impediments developing from circumstances of this program planning process. This degree program was pursued beyond each partner institution's traditional forms of international engagement; thus, some noteworthy obstacles were encountered.

First, for the Singaporean institution, a new model of international collaboration was essential in order to clear away the previous taint of colonial patterns left behind by some unequal international programming of the past. Administrators on both sides of the partnership had to demonstrate a commitment to equal collaboration through meetings and negotiations involving the faculty on the Singapore side of the arrangement. The face-to-face conference held in Singapore did much to unite the two partner institutions and spawned research collaborations that continue. Any hint that this partnership might be relying on previous unequal patterns of international programming was an initial barrier to this program.

Yet, for the US side to accept the Singaporean institution as an equal partner was also a hindrance to adoption of this pioneering program model. While the participating faculty and administrators from the Chemical Engineering department were supportive of the program, in a decentralized system such as the US Land-grant research institution model, committees from across campus must understand, approve, and ratify the program. Moreover, university and then state governing boards must also approve the program since it involves the issuance of a shared diploma. As expressed by some participants, sharing the diploma raised concerns about protecting the "brand" of the US institution as well as linking the institution in a collaborative degree. Because of the US university's tradition of localism, stakeholders also expressed concerns that the program would somehow be diverting resources from local students and programs, or would seem to be diverting such resources and, thus, would attract negative local attention. Because this collaboration broke with established patterns of operation developed out of traditions such as localism, it required more explanation and justification than might otherwise have been expected.

Taken together, these situations reveal the challenges and potential barriers of establishing new models responsive to the global network of higher education. As institutions strive to reposition themselves outside of strictly development or market driven models, the process of developing an international program can be hampered, slowed. Such findings seem to confirm Delanty's position, that to function effectively as a mediator of discourses in the knowledge society, the current structure of the university would have to be significantly altered (2001). In a global network that seems to value nimble process and quick adaptations, the US land-grant research institution is in the unfamiliar position of being disadvantaged by its size and processes. Of course, some administrators have argued, and rightly so, that it is those very processes that have made the US system the model for the world. At issue now is whether large bureaucratic research institutions, in many ways the birthplace of modern global science, can continue to compete when quick adaptations seem to be advantageous in the global networks in which they function. The former Dean of Engineering captured the ethos that has informed the US higher education system when he defended this planning model by explaining that "the process should not be evaluated for speed. There is no non-destructive test on a student's education. We must, therefore, be very careful..." (personal communication, February 25, 2009). This case illustrates the conflict between careful development and the global demands in international programming in higher education and in global science.

IP protection is also a significant barrier to overcome in the process of developing this collaboration. Singapore's recent adaptation of IP law does much to mitigate its history as the "piracy capital of the world." Nevertheless, according to the Director for International Partnerships at Midwestern, negotiations surrounding IP rights presented the biggest challenge to the partnership. As described in chapter three, since the Bayh-Dole Act of 1980, US universities retain the rights of intellectual property developed by their faculty. Under this partnership, those rights would need to be shared as well as protected. Campus Legal Counsel for Midwestern university explained that much of the work was trailblazing, as it was beyond the scope of typical arrangements. First, the joint ownership that this partnership necessitated is "completely different from our usual work in IP" (personal communication, March 18, 2009) requiring joint ownership and potentially joint licensing. Second, protecting IP rights internationally would be more challenging than protecting IP domestically. Though IP issues were eventually negotiated to both parties' specifications, "that part took the longest of all to negotiate," according to the Director for International Partnerships at Midwestern university (personal communication, March 12, 2009). The importance of IP rights demonstrates the growing overlap between global higher education networks and the network of global science. Moreover, it suggests the worldwide reach of the academic-industry partnerships that flow through such networks.

Cultural conditions also presented significant barriers to overcome. Despite shared language and shared goals between Midwestern university and Singapore university, program planners were still forced to negotiate through cultural divides representing differences in values as well as procedures. Though a number of Singaporean administrators had been educated in the US system, and though Singapore was in many ways forming its institutional practices after the US model, differences in research style, governance structures, and productivity measures all presented as barriers to the process.

Perhaps most notable of the cultural divides from the US institution's perspective was Singapore's reliance on key performance indicators, or KPIs. Several participants on the US side of the collaboration expressed frustration with Singapore's tendency to reduce the program to measurable numbers evident in KPIs. As has been demonstrated, KPIs present perhaps the biggest threat to the continuation of the program as failing to meet KPIs has led to other international program closures in Singapore. Moreover KPIs represent the ability of Singapore to assert its own cultural form into the program and to exhibit a measure of control over the planning process and the functioning of the program.

Potentialities.

Despite these significant barriers, a number of noteworthy potentialities presented by this innovation can be appreciated as a result of this study.

First, the hierarchal commercialized model of international education has become more fluid and complex with the repositioning now possible through the global network of higher education. While shadows of hierarchy and markets outlined are still evident, new models of international programming are emerging that flatten the hierarchy to some extent for some institutions and deemphasize the role of markets. Previously, globally networked institutions were concentrated in the US specifically and the West in general, with international engagement serving a developmental function or as a market driven conduit for largely one-sided financial gain. In this study, however, the Singaporean institution is able to shift hierarchal status as well as derive its own significant gain through the partnership. Moreover, in contrast to the development focused programs of the past, it is the US institution that is seeking access to state of the art facilities and exposure to wider research opportunities.

This study illustrates that through global network membership, hierarchy and markets are potentially de-emphasized and increasingly fluid. For example, due to the growing recognition of the importance of global network membership, particularly for chemical engineering, each side of the partnership exerted push/pull factors, directing the program's development. While the US institution requires world-class facilities and IP protection, Singapore is also able to assert its own requirements into the collaboration through the reliance on KPIs as well as through providing funding incentives. Both sides of the collaboration instituted requirements that became a part of the shared code of communication linking the institutions in this degree program.

Moreover, both institutions will be equally represented on the diploma or seal that students receive at the end of the program. As we have seen in chapters five and six, this represents a significant compromise on the part of some administrators and faculty at the US institution and symbolizes acceptance of the Singaporean institution as a comparable partner. For Singapore, this symbolizes the institution's ascendancy beyond the colonial patterns of some past international programming to the status of a full participating member in an international partnership with a world-class institution.

While we cannot say that based on this one case, the US institution is moving into a completely non-competitive mode of international collaboration beyond market strategies, we can find that this type of collaboration represents at the very least the potential for a new kind of competitive strategy; one that recognizes the importance of global network membership and global partnerships. Moreover, because the US stands to gain both financially and from the perspective of facilities and research potential, this global partner cannot be viewed as strictly a recipient of aid, or strictly as a potential market, but must be acknowledged as a worthy collaborator evidenced in the shared seal on the diploma of the program. For Singapore, we cannot find that the shackles of a post-colonial identity have been completely cast aside so that it can function equally on the international stage; however, we can say that this program development has demonstrated the potential for Singapore to establish new patterns of engagement beyond its colonial past.

Clearly, the new social structure outlined by Castells and Appadurai allows the potential disruption in previous forms of international engagement to make new forms of collaboration such as this multi-institutional degree viable. Rather than a unitary sense of global order, networks flow in all directions and are not oriented or organized around a controlling source. The new social structure of network society creates the possibility for new patterns of social organization, even if under the shadow of hierarchy and markets.

Despite the US higher education's overwhelming dominance evident in the isomorphism of US models around the globe, current developments in Singapore suggest that such dominance is fluid as well. Singapore's newest university, Singapore University of Technology and Design, is established in collaboration with MIT, which follows the predictable hierarchal models we might expect, yet it is also developed with Zhejiang University in China, suggesting another shift in the tides of global higher education. Singapore University of Technology and Design is meant to serve as an education laboratory with engineering as the focus. The new institution is guided by a mission of taking on real-world problems and quickly moving research from the lab to the marketplace (Young, 2010). The link to China may signal the flow of the network spreading outward, moving beyond strict hierarchal patterns or this partnership may indicate a shift in the hierarchy with China rising to a stronger position. At any rate, the link between MIT, Zhejiang University, and Singapore University of Technology and Design in the field of engineering education further reveals the fluid nature of power and influence in the global networks of education and science.

Second, this study reveals the potential for nation states, local institutions and even individuals to "pick and choose the ways in which, and the degree to which they can participate in a global world" (Burbules & Torres, 2000, p. 17). Clearly, national contexts and national policies still play an enormous role in directing the flows within the global network of higher education. Throughout this case, the Singaporean government has been a driving force. The US government has played a role as well, though perhaps in an unintended way, through its discontinuation of funding. Cuts in state budgets as well as stipulations in federal funding regarding international engagement both served to spur the US institution to pursue international partnerships.

But it is not only the nation state directing the flows, as both institutions have exercised agency as well. Both institutions were able to extend their traditional patterns of international engagement and collaborate on a new model of international program making use of, but not being limited by, the global network of higher education. This study makes clear the potentialities for institutions to choose the way in which they will participate in the global network.

Also, this study highlights the importance of individual social networks which became as important in this case as the electronic connections that facilitate them. Without the face-to-face interactions, shared research, and ongoing social and professional connections between key administrators and faculty on both campuses, the many barriers to this program may have impeded its progress, or derailed the program completely. This program demonstrates the continued potentiality of individual relationships and personal networks to direct the connectivity within the global network of higher education.

Next, this study reveals the potential for disruption in the nationally based triple helix of university-industry-government relations (Etzkowitz & Leydesdorff, 1997). As participants stated, the funding provided by the Singaporean government and other Singaporean funding agencies has allowed what Castells has called the "de-localiz[ation] of production from its country basis, and shifts it to multi-locational, global networks" (2009, p. 129). In this way, science, specifically in this case, the field of chemical engineering, could free itself from prevailing dependency on US federal funding that has dominated and, some would argue, dictated the direction of development particularly in the post-WWII era (Leslie, 1993; Paarlberg, 2004). This may allow for a potential resurgence of science driven by intellectual curiosity and an uncorrupted pursuit of knowledge for engineering faculty and their students. Alternatively, such funding could be only another source of domination from a foreign state and its own networked multi-national corporations. In short, are we to see the diversity of research interests now possible through Singapore's petroleum processing as a liberation from project allocations of the US federal government, thus creating new potentialities in the network of global science? Or, is this a new "mobilization" on behalf of a "better funded" government with better funded partners in MNCs?

Further, what are the potentialities for the results of research directed from Singapore? Like Dumas (1984), who finds that there are possible positive effects of technological innovations developed originally with military purpose and funding, we might suppose that there will be positive spin-offs for the US beyond strictly profit. Yet the concerns raised by Dumas about military research could similarly be raised about research directed by the Singaporean state. Singapore is also frequently characterized as "a highly authoritarian system," with "inherent values . . . at odds with the principles of personal freedom, individuality and pursuit of enlightened self-interest, the ideals of the wider body of society in the US" (Dumas, 1984, p. 145). The potentialities for conflicting research agendas between institutions situated with such differing societal cultures seem quite possible.

Moreover, what is the potential for creative innovation within such a system? While the Singaporean government aims to import innovation and creativity, could it be, as some critics have suggested, that creativity cannot function in a restrictive environment? Will innovation in engineers and engineering education flourish in an environment that is frequently characterized as conformist, standardized, and lacking in academic freedoms? If the Singaporean government is able to import this culture of creation and innovation, then this program may represent the beginning of new potentialities in global science, yet if this social and political experiment fails, this program may signal a net loss in creativity in science education and a corresponding loss for global science.

At any rate, it seems clear that the "golden triangle" of military agencies, high technology industry, and research universities has become more complex, with the triangle replaced by a complex web of "multi-locational global networks" (Castells, 2009, p. 129). While some view this shift as a potential threat to US dominance and, consequently, US and global security (Paarlberg, 2004), one could also view this as a rupture creating potentialities by allowing other interests to compete for scientists' creative attention. This complex web may create the potential for new influences within the emerging network of global science.

Implications obviously extend well beyond the network of engineering universities to impact the field of engineering and the potential careers of engineers. On the one hand, offshoring of engineering creates an expanded market for engineering skills. For example, some have argued that long term benefits accrue to the US as other nations, such as India and China, develop and thereby increase the need for engineers as living standards and the demands of society rise. However, on the other hand, companies will then be able to shop for lower wages by moving engineering operations to favorable locations. Of course, it may be that engineers themselves can continue to command value in the global marketplace by being more mobile themselves than the corporations that employ them (National Academy of Engineering, 2008). As engineering continues to be pushed and pulled in global flows, engineers and engineering students will be similarly affected.

Finally, this case contributes to the discussion of the future for the university, specifically the potentiality for the university to function as what Delanty has called a hub of interconnectivity in the knowledge society (2001). As we saw in chapter two, Delanty casts the potential future of the university as a mediator among discourses. Delanty locates the central task of the twenty-first century university to become a key actor in the public sphere capable of mediating among the production of knowledge as a set of discourses cutting across institutional and epistemological forms. Not the hegemon of center to periphery constructions, or the reproducer of neoliberalism's agenda dedicated to free markets and a minimal state, but existing as a hub or node in the networked knowledge society.

In this case study, the partner universities' development of the multi-institutional degree demonstrates exactly that potential for the university to function as a primary node or hub of interconnectivity in global networks of the knowledge society that include higher education as well as global science. Just as the harbors once served as the primary hubs of interconnectivity around the globe in the era of global shipping networks, the universities in this case express the university's potential to transcend the limitations and patterns of the "self-referential bureaucratic organization" (Delanty, 2001, p. 17) and become the hub of interconnectivity in the global networks of knowledge exemplified in this multi-institutional degree. Despite the lengthy negotiations, stalled processes, halting progress and the current uneven status of the final approved program, the development of a new form of international education program at the PhD level across institutional, national, and cultural lines is an enormous attainment indicating a new potential level of connectivity in the global arena of higher education. Given the central position of research universities in the knowledge society, such connectivity will necessarily have ramifications on global science, as we have seen, as well as in numerous other realms. Moreover, given the worldwide status and regional importance of the partner institutions, it is likely that this connectivity, and the negotiations that inform it, will be replicated and then further vernacularized in numerous configurations around the globe. The potentials created by this new form of international program are then, in these ways, endless.

Considerations for Further Research

This study indicates a number of points for further research. First, while it is apparent that this program was developed in response to global trends, it is unclear to what extent multi-institutional degrees represent an emerging form in international programming. While the US institution was pioneering in its adoption of a shared degree, the Singaporean institution was involved in several other joint degree programs, suggesting regional differences in the reliance on such multi-institutional programs. Further studies are needed in order to place this program form clearly within emerging global trends.

Second, similar case studies from different disciplines would help to distinguish between factors that are specific to the sciences and engineering and those that are cross-disciplinary in nature. For example, case studies on programs in the humanities, arts or social sciences would add perspective to issues of brand management, IP rights, and funding concerns, all of which played determining roles in this particular program planning. Also, similar studies situated within institutions from different nationalities would also add to this developing line of research (see Marginson & Sawir, 2005; Luke & Luke, 2000)

Next, much research is needed in order to understand the relationship between international education and the global network of science. While it is clear that the US national "golden triangle" has been disrupted, at least in terms of its previously national emphasis, the impact and potentials exposed can only begin to be explored here. As we have seen, the introduction of the fourth strand of international collaboration into the golden triangle may break the potentially corrupting power of the structure. Alternatively it may simply buttress the power of the industry helix while replicating this model around the globe.

Finally, issues related to "brain drain" have only been touched on in this study, but in connection with the overlap between international education networks and the global network of science, questions concerning the mobility of scientists and scholars arise. This case seems to present a counter trend to what has been the norm in the post-war era. Previously, both international education and science created a synergy that brought the world's brightest students, scholars and scientists to the US laboratories and research universities. In this case, however, the final program is for Singaporean students, and while those students will graduate with the credential from a prestigious US research university, they will do so with less time in the US, less time in a US laboratory, and with less direction from US faculty than a traditional degree program situated in the US would require. Moreover, two top administrators from the US university, from the sciences no less, were recruited to Singapore university during the development of this program. These factors suggest that the flow of scientists and scholars primarily to the US may be shifting. Much further research is needed to determine the extent and ramifications of such potential shifts.

Conclusion

The central research questions of this case considered the nature of collaboration between a large US Midwestern research institution and a rapidly growing research institution in Singapore. Because of the dominance of US higher education and corresponding isomorphism around the globe in conjunction with Singapore's colonial history and position at the gateway to Asian markets, we might expect that the terms of the program would flow from center to periphery, with a dominant US institution dictating and directing the program's form and function. Indeed, the isomorphism found globally is typically attributed to a center to periphery flows of power with neoliberal agendas directing the flows.

However, this study discovers that the flows are multi-directional and, thus, unpredictable. In this case, the initial conception and much of the impetus originated in Singapore. In fact, this program was first imagined in the Singapore harbor amidst staggering economic growth and accompanying demands. Even at the US institution, the driving force was always from those with the strongest connections to Singapore in time spent there and in the personal relationships maintained from there. Clearly, the collaboration was perpetually driven forward by the Singaporean institution and government. Further evidence demonstrates that the program was directly in line with Singaporean government policies as a part of its push to become a global hub in education and global science through appropriation of some key facets of US models.

Yet, education is a cultural form. To copy its operating systems, even value systems, will not automatically result in an exact replica. Unlike a music recording pirated to make an exact duplication, the cultural form of education will result in a "glocalization," a blend of global and local forms. This appropriation more accurately approximates the willing and purposeful adoption of English language, now termed "Singlish" in Singapore to capture the many idioms and indigenization that the Singaporean language has imbued in it. The higher education culture, too, will indigenize, and likely continue to spread and further indigenize throughout the region. Within each hybridization small shifts occur. While at this time, it seems that much of the US system has been reproduced, "glocalization" occurs in centrally unpredictable ways.

This study suggests that, while not entirely flat, the hierarchical relationships that have characterized international higher education are shifting. In order for the social structure to move from a hierarchal arrangement to a more evenly dispersed network form, the power must reconfigure, spread out, and flow between the nodes. At the moment of this shift, we could expect that the concentric circles would first spread outwards and then flow back towards their source, creating waves and counter waves in an almost indiscernible current. This study seems to capture that moment of shift for the two partner institutions. Though the study begins with the traditional hierarchy in place, through the negotiation of the collaboration, the network ties are strengthened, and the hierarchy gives way. The resulting waves of give and take trace the flow of power amidst the current of global processes and demands. Examining the rationales, barriers and potentialities that emerge in the planning process of a multi-institutional degree finds both sides of the academic partnership exercising agency in the push-pull stream of global flows. Therefore, this study does not follow a post-colonial narrative or a narrative of center to periphery, American hegemony. Within this case study, there is no clear privileged center, nor resistance to hegemony at the local level on the periphery.

Instead, from the vantage point of this case, the global network of higher education has afforded a partnership that on one side allows a powerful state-driven agenda to flourish, while at the same time, on the other side, fills financial and policy gaps in an overburdened, bureaucratized, locally governed education system. In fact, evidence suggests that both partner institutions shared the goal of demonstrating membership in the global network of higher education through the degree program and partnership. Moreover, both partner institutions introduce requirements that must be negotiated and adhered to for the collaboration to function. Contrary to neo-liberal narratives of globalization that highlight the "runaway train" power of supranational organizations engaged in an agenda dedicated to free market individualism and a minimal state, or narratives that portray global forces moving from center to periphery, this study highlights the important role that national government, local government and even individuals play in determining the form that the global network will take in local institutions. While global network membership is valued, narratives of globalization are recruited to serve local goals, specific to local institutions and their stakeholders. Paradoxically, this study finds globalization narratives recruited to serve both nation state and local agendas. The negotiations between these agendas are carried out by individuals whose personal relationships strengthen the ties of the collaboration and form a network that ultimately spans the globe as well as generations.

Because of the specificity of this case study, the findings are, therefore, specific, yet the study provides a counter narrative to the center to periphery constructions and adds complexity to the status of isomorphic US higher education models found around the globe. This study illuminates the value of examining particular places, incorporating diverse local experience into the narrative of the network society.

Bibliography

Afolayan, M. & Witt, M.A. (2010). Capitalism in the Theatre of Democracy. *Learning for Democracy.* 4(1).

Altbach, P. (1998). *Comparative Higher Education: Knowledge, the University, and Development.* Greenwood.

─── (2001). Higher Education and the WTO: Globalization Run Amok. *International Higher Education, Spring 2001.* Retrieved from http://www.universitetoplum.org/text.php3?id=19

─── (2004a). Globalisation and the University: Myths and Realities in an Unequal World. *Tertiary Education and Management, 10*(1), 3-25.

─── (2004b). Higher Education Crosses Borders. *Change, 36*(2), 18-24.

─── (2007). Empires of Knowledge and Development. In P. G. Altbach & J. Balan (Eds.), *World Class Worldwide: Transforming Research Universities in Asia and Latin America.* Baltimore, MD: Johns Hopkins University Press.

Altbach, P., Gumport, P. J., & Johnstone, B. (2001). *In Defense of American Higher Education.* Baltimore, MD: Johns Hopkins University Press.

Altbach, P. & Knight, J. (2007). The Internationalization of Higher Education: Motivations and Realities. *Journal of Studies in International Education, 11*(3), 290-305.

Appadurai, A. (1996). *Modernity at Large: Cultural Dimensions of Globalization.* Minneapolis, MN: University of Minnesota Press.

─── (2001). Grassroots Globalization and the Research Imagination. In Appadurai, A. (Ed.). *Globalization.* Durham, NC: Duke University Press.

Atkinson, P., Coffey, A., & Delamont, S. (2003). *Key Themes in Qualitative Research.* New York, NY: AltaMira Press.

Bain, O., & Cummings, W. (2005). Where Have the International Students Gone? *International Educator*, 14(2), 18-26.

Balan, J. (2007). Higher Education Policy and the Research University. In P. Altbach & J. Balan (Eds.), *World Class Worldwide: Transforming Research Universities in Asia and Latin America.* Baltimore, MD: Johns Hopkins University Press.

Bartell, M. (2003). Internationalization of Universities: A University Culture-based Framework. *Higher Education, 45*(1), 43-70.

Bauman, Z. (1998). *Globalization: The Human Consequences.* New York, NY: Columbia University Press.

─── (1998). On Glocalization: Or Globalization for Some, Localization for Some Others. *Thesis Eleven, 54*(1), 37-49.

─── (2002). *Society Under Siege.* Cambridge, England, Polity Press.

Beerkens, E., & Derwende, M. (2007). The Paradox in International Cooperation: Institutionally Embedded Universities in a Global Environment. *Higher Education: The International Journal of Higher Education and Educational Planning, 53*(1), 61-79.

Bernardo, A. B. (2003). International Higher Education: Models, Conditions and Issues. In T. S. Tullao (Ed.), *Education and Globalization*. Makiti City, Philippines: Philippine Institute for Development Studies.

Bourdieu, P. (1988). *Homo Academicus*. Cambridge, England: Polity Press.

——— (1994). *Reproduction in Education, Society and Culture*. London, England: Sage.

——— (1996). *The State Nobility: Elite Schools in the Field of Power*. Stanford, CA: Stanford University Press.

Bourdieu, P., & Passeron, J. (1996). *Reproduction in Education, Society and Culture*. London, England: Sage.

Bourdieu, P., & Wacquant, L. (1999). On the Cunning of Imperialist Reason. *Theory, Culture & Society*, *16*(1), 41-58.

Bradsher, K. (2009, May 13). Ships Tread Water, Waiting for Cargo - NYTimes.com. Retrieved from http://www.nytimes.com/2009/05/13/business/global/13ship.html

Brubacher, J., & Rudy, W. (1997). *Higher Education in Transition: A History of American Colleges and Universities*. New Brunswick, NJ: Transaction Publishers.

Burbules, N., & Torres, C. A. (2000). Globalization and Education: an introduction. In N. C. Burbules & C. A. Torres (Eds.), *Globalization and Education: Critical Perspectives*. New York, NY: Routledge.

Castells, M. (1999). *Information Technology, Globalization, and Social Development*. United Nations Research Institute for Social Development (UNRISD), Geneva, Switzerland.

——— (2002). Local and Global: Cities in the Network Society. *Tijdschrift voor Economische en Sociale Geografie*, *93*(5), 548-558.

——— (2004). *The Power of Identity*. Malden, MA: Blackwell.

——— (2009). *The Rise of the Network Society*. Malden, MA: Blackwell.

Chan, R. (2009, September 26). Jurong Isle to Get New Facilities; New barge terminal, second road coming up. *The Straits Times (Singapore)*.

Chomsky, N. (1999). *Profit Over People: Neoliberalism and Global Order*. New York, NY: Seven Stories Press.

Clark, D. L., & Astuto, T. A. (1989). The Disjunction of Federal Educational Policy and National Educational Needs in the 1990s. *Journal of Education Policy*, *4*(5).

Clark, I. (1997). *Globalization and Fragmentation: International Relations in the Twentieth Century*. Oxford, England: Oxford University Press.

Clarke, D. (2003). *The Consumer Society and the Postmodern City*. London: Routledge.

Considine, M., Marginson, S., Sheehan, P., & Kumnick, M. (2001). *The Comparative Performance of Australia as a Knowledge Nation*. Melbourne, Australia: Chifley Research Centre.

Dale, R. (2000). Globalization and Education: Demonstrating a "Common World Educational Culture" or Locating a "Globally Structured Educational Agenda"? *Educational Theory*, *50*(4), 427-48.

Deem, R. (2001). Globalisation, New Managerialism, Academic Capitalism and Entrepreneurialism in Universities: Is the Local Dimension Still Important? *Comparative Education*, *37*(1), 7-20.

Deem, R., Mok, K. H., & Lucas, L. (2008). Transforming Higher Education in Whose Image? Exploring the Concept of the World-Class University in Europe and Asia. *Higher Education Policy*, *21*, 83-97.

Delanty, G. (1998). The Idea of the University in the Global Era: From Human as an End to the End of Knowledge? *Social Epistemology*, *12*(1), 3-26.

——— (2001). *Challenging Knowledge: The University in the Knowledge Society*. Buckingham, UK: Society for Research into Higher Education.
deWit, H. (2002). *Internationalization of Higher Education in the United States of America and Europe: A Historical, Comparative, and Conceptual Analysis*. Westport CT: Greenwood Press.
Douglas, J. (1976). *Investigative Social Research*. Beverly Hills, CA: Sage.
——— (2005). *All Globalization is Local: Countervailing Forces and the Influence on Higher Education Markets* (No. CSHE.1.05). Research & Occasional Paper Series. Center for Studies in Higher Education: University of California, Berkeley.
Dumas, L. L. (1984). University Research, Industrial Innovation, and the Pentagon. In J. Tirman (Ed.), *The Militarization of High Technology*. Cambridge, MA: Ballinger.
Economic Review Committee, Ministry of Trade and Industry, Singapore. (2002). Ministry of Trade and Industry: ERC Reports. Retrieved September 26, 2010, from http://app.mti.gov.sg/default.asp?id=507
Erikson, F. (1986). *Qualitative Methods in Research on Teaching*. In M.C. Wittrock (Ed.) *Handbook on Research on Teaching* (pp. 119-161). New York, NY: Macmillan.
Etzkowitz, H., & Leydesdorff, L. (Eds.). (1997a). *Universities and the Global Knowledge Economy: A Triple Helix of University-Industry-Government Relations*. New York, NY: Pinter.
Feldman, J. (1989). Economic Conversion: An Alternative to Military Dependency in the University. *Annals of the New York Academy of Sciences, 577* (Ethical Issues Associated with Scientific and Technological Research for the Military), 231-241.
Frank, D., & Gabler, J. (2006). *Restructuring the University: Worldwide Shifts in Academia in the 20th Century*. Stanford CA: Stanford University Press.
Freeman, R. B. (2005). Does Globalization of the Scientific/Engineering Workforce Threaten U.S. Economic Leadership? *SSRN eLibrary*. Retrieved from http://papers.ssrn.com/sol3/papers.cfm?abstract_id=755693.
Friedmann, J., & Hudson, B. (1974). Knowledge and Action: A Guide to Planning Theory. *Journal of the American Planning Association, 40*(1), 2.
Fulbright, W. J. (1970). Science and the Universities in the Military-Industrial Complex. In Schiller, H., & Phillips, J. D. (Eds.). *Super-State Readings in the Military-Industrial Complex*. Urbana: University of Illinois Press.
Garrett, R. (2003). *Transnational Higher Education, Part 1: The Major Markets - Hong Kong & Singapore*. The Observatory on Borderless Higher Education.
Geertz, C. (1973). *The Interpretation of Cultures: Selected Essays*. New York, NY: Basic Books.
Gibbons, M. (1995). *The New Production of Knowledge the Dynamics of Science and Research in Contemporary Societies*. London, UK: Sage.
Giddens, A. (1990). *Social Theory Today*. Cambridge, UK: Polity.
——— (2003). *Runaway World: How Globalization is Reshaping Our Lives*. New York, NY: Routledge.
Glazer, N. (1970). *Remembering the Answers: Essays on the American Student Revolt*. New York, NY: Basic Books.
Gonzalez, R. J. (2007). We Must Fight the Militarization of Anthropology. *Chronicle of Higher Education, 53*(22).

Goudie, C. (2006, March 27). Why We Need to Fight the University of Illinois' Foreign Policy. *Chicago Daily Herald*, 15.

Green, M., & Olson, C. (2003). *Internationalizing the Campus: A User's Guide*. Washington, DC: American Council on Education, Center for Institutional and International Initiatives.

Green, Robert, & Gerber, L. (1997). Toward Global Education: Strategic Partnerships with Overseas Institutions. *Selections*, 13(2), 32-40.

Guba, E.G., & Lincoln, Y.S. (1981). *Effective Evaluation*. London, UK: Jossey-Bass.

Gürüz, K. (2008). *Higher Education and International Student Mobility in the Global Knowledge Economy*. Albany: State University of New York Press.

Hannah, S. B. (1996). The Higher Education Act of 1992: Skills, Constraints, and the Politics of Higher Education. *Journal of Higher Education*, 67(5), 598-627.

Harding, A., Scott, A., Laske, S., & Burtscher, C. (Eds.). (2007). *Bright Satanic Mills: Universities, Regional Development and the Knowledge Economy*. Aldershot, UK: Ashgate.

Held, D. (2003). *The Global Transformations Reader: An Introduction to the Globalization Debate*. Malden, UK: Polity Press.

Hill, M., & Lian, K. F. (1995). *The Politics of Nation Building and Citizenship in Singapore*. New York, NY: Routledge.

Hirst, P. Q. (1996). *Globalization in Question: The International Economy and the Possibilities of Governance*. Cambridge, UK: Polity Press.

Hoong, C. M. (2007, May 26). Lessons from the University Fallout; S'pore Agencies Should Look at Recent Failures in Joint Ventures to Avoid Future Fiascos. *The Straits Times (Singapore)*.

Horsky, B., & Ghim-Lian Chew, P. (2004). Singapore: Schools in the Service of Society. In I. C. Rotberg (Ed.), *Balancing Change and Tradition in Global Education Reform*. Lanham, Md.: Rowan & Littlefield.

Institute of International Education. (1989). Open Doors. New York, NY: Institute of International Education.

Jantsch, E. (1972). *Technological Planning and Social Futures*. New York, NY: Wiley.

Jayasuriya, K. (2001). Globalization, Sovereignty, and the Rule of Law: From Political to Economic Constitutionalism? *Constellations*, 8(4), 442-460.

Kaghan, W. N., & Barnett, G. B. (1997). The Desktop Model of Innovation in Digital Media. In H. Etzkowitz & L. Leydesdorff (Eds.), *Universities and the Global Knowledge Economy: A Triple Helix of University-Industry-Government Relations*. New York, NY: Pinter.

Kapitzke, C., & Hay, S. (2008). Gateways to the Global: Governing School-Industry Partnerships. Conference Paper. Retrieved from http://eprints.qut.edu.au/10576/.

Kapur, D. (2007). The Economic Impact of International Migration from India. In *Movement of Global Talent: The Impact of High Skill Labor Flows from India and China* (pp. 23-34). Princeton, NJ: Woodrow Wilson School of Public and International Affairs, Princeton University.

Kerr, C. (1991). International Learning and National Purposes in Higher Education. *American Behavioral Scientist*, 35(1), 17-42.

——— (1991). *The Great Transformation in Higher Education, 1960-1980*. Albany: State University of New York Press.

Khondker, H. (2004). Glocalization as Globalization: Evolution of a Sociological Concept. *Bangladesh e-Journal of Sociology*, 1(2), 1-9.

Knight, J. (2003). *GATS, Trade and Higher Education. Perspective 2003—Where Are We?*, 2-29. Retrieved from http://www.obhe.ac.uk.

Kofman, E., & Youngs, G. (Eds.). (2003). *Globalization: Theory and Practice*. London, UK: Continuum.

Koh, A. (2004). Singapore Education in "New Times": Global/local Imperatives. *Discourse: Studies in the Cultural Politics of Education, 25*(3), 335-49.

Krathwohl, D. (1998). *Methods of Educational & Social Science Research: An Integrated Approach*. New York, NY: Longman.

Langan, E. (2004). France & the United States: the Competition for University Students Bologna and Beyond. *Higher Education Policy, 17*(4).

Lee, M. H. (2008). University Restructuring in Singapore: Amazing or a Maze? *Policy Futures in Education, 6*(5), 569-588.

Leslie, S. W. (1993). *The Cold War and American Science: The Military-Industrial-Academic Complex at MIT and Stanford*. New York, NY: Columbia University Press.

Lim, T. (1995). Malaysian and Singaporean Higher Education: Common Roots but Differing Directions. In A. H. Yee (Ed.), *East Asian Higher Education: Traditions and Transformations*. New York, NY: Pergamon.

Lingard, B., Rawolle, S., & Taylor, S. (2005). Globalizing Policy Sociology in Education: Working with Bourdieu. *Journal of Education Policy, 20*(6), 759-777.

Lucas, C. (1994). *American Higher Education: A history*. New York, NY: St. Martin's Press.

Lucas, R. (2001). *Diaspora and Development: Highly Skilled Migrants from East Asia* (pp. 1-49). Boston University. Retrieved from http://web.bu.edu/econ/ied/dp/papers/dp120.pdf.

Luke, A., & Luke, C. (2000). A Situated Perspective on Cultural Globalization. In N. C. Burbules & C. A. Torres (Eds.), *Globalization and Education: Critical Perspectives*. New York, NY: Routledge.

Maclean, J. (2000). Review Essay: Globalization and the Failure of the Sociological Imagination: a Review essay. *Critical Sociology, 26*(3), 329-349.

Marginson, S. (1995). Markets in Education: A Theoretical Note. *Australian Journal of Education, 39*(3), 294-312.

——— (2000). Rethinking Academic Work in the Global Era. *Journal of Higher Education Policy & Management, 22*(1), 23-35.

——— (2004). Bright Networks and Dark Spaces. *Academe, 90*(3), 37-41.

Marginson, S., & Rhoades, G. (2002). Beyond National States, Markets, and Systems of Higher Education: A Glonacal Agency Heuristic. *Higher Education, 43*(3), 281-309.

Marginson, S., & Sawir, E. (2005). Interrogating Global Flows in Higher Education. *Globalisation, Societies and Education, 3*(3), 281-309.

Meredith, R. (2007). *The Elephant and the Dragon: The Rise of India and China and What It Means for All of Us*. New York, NY: W.W. Norton.

Morrow, R. A., & Torres, C. A. (2000). The State, Globalization, and Educational Policy. In N. C. Burbules & C. A. Torres (Eds.), *Globalization and Education: Critical Perspectives*. New York, NY: Routledge.

Ministry of Education Singapore. (2001). Retrieved from http://www.moe.gov.sg.

Mohrman, K., Ma, W., & Baker, D. (2008). The Research University in Transition: The Emerging Global Model. *Higher Education Policy, 21*(1), 5-27.

Mok, K. H. (2000). Impact of Globalization: A Study of Quality Assurance Systems of Higher Education in Hong Kong and Singapore. *Comparative Education Review, 44*(2).

——— (2008). Singapore's Global Education Hub Ambitions: University Governance Change and Transnational Higher Education. *International Journal of Educational Management, 22*(6), 527-546.

Montsion, J. M. (2009). Relocating Politics at the Gateway: Everyday Life in Singapore's Global Schoolhouse. *Pacific Affairs, 82*(4), 637-656.

National Academy of Engineering. (2008). NAE Website - Offshoring Engineering Facts, Myths, Unknowns, and Implications. Retrieved online from http://www.nae.edu/Activities/Projects20676/OffshoringEngineering.aspx.

Nederveen Pieterse, J. (2004). *Globalization or Empire?* New York, NY: Routledge.

Nelson, R. R., & Wright, G. (1992). The Rise and Fall of American Technological Leadership: The Postwar Era in Historical Perspective. *Journal of Economic Literature, 30*(4), 1931-1964.

Newman, F., Couturier, L. & Scurry, J. (2004). *The Future of Higher Education: Rhetoric, Reality, and the Risks of the Market.* San Francisco, CA: Jossey-Bass.

Ngenda, A. (2005). The Nature of the International Intellectual Property System: Universal Norms and Values or Western Chauvinism? *Information & Communications Technology Law, 14*(1), 59.

Nisbet, R. (1971). *The Degradation of the Academic Dogma: The University in America, 1945-1970.* New York, NY: Basic Books.

Obstfield M. & Taylor, A. (2003). Sovereign Risk, Credibility and the Gold Standard. *The Economic Journal.* 113(487), 241-275.

Olds, K. (2007). Global Assemblage: Singapore, Foreign Universities, and the Construction of a "Global Education Hub." *World Development, 35*(6), 959-975.

Olds, K., & Thrift, N. (2005). Assembling the 'Global Schoolhouse' in Pacific Asia: The Case of Singapore. In P. Daniels, K. Ho, & T. Hutton (Eds.), *Service Industries and Asia-Pacific Cities: New Development Trajectories.* London, UK: Routledge.

Paarlberg, R. L. (2004). Knowledge as Power: Science, Military Dominance, and U.S. Security. *International Security, 29*(1), 122-151.

Peters, M. (2006). The Rise of Global Science and the Emerging Political Economy of International Research Collaborations. *European Journal of Education, 41*(2), 225-244.

——— (2009). *The Changing Architecture of Global Science* (Occasional Paper No. 7). Center for Global Studies: University of Illinois at Urbana-Champaign. Retrieved from http://hdl.handle.net/2142/10682.

Pierson, P. (1998). Irresistible Forces, Immovable Objects: Post-industrial Welfare States Confront Permanent Austerity. *Journal of European Public Policy, 5*(4), 539-560.

Powell, W. (1990). Neither Market nor Hierarchy: Network Forms of Organization. *Research in Organizational Behavior, 12*, 295-335.

Purnell, N. (2010). A Singapore University Plans its First Residential Colleges. *Chronicle of Higher Education.* December 14, 2010. Retrieved from http://chronicle.com.

Qiang, Z. (2003). Internationalization of Higher Education: Towards a conceptual framework. *Policy Futures in Education, 1*(2), 248-70.

Ramcharan, R. (2006). Singapore's Emerging Knowledge Economy: Role of Intellectual Property and Its Possible Implications for Singaporean Society. *The Journal of World Intellectual Property, 9*(3), 316-343.

Reichert, S., & Wachter, B. (2000). *Globalisation of Education and Training: Recommendations for a Coherent Response to the European Union.* Brussels, Belgium: European Commission.

Rhoads, R. A. (2003). Globalization and Resistance in the United States and Mexico: The Global Potemkin Village. *Higher Education, 45*(2), 223-50.

Ritzer, G. (2004). *The McDonaldization of Society*. Thousand Oaks, CA: Pine Forge Press.

Rizvi, F. (2004). Debating Globalization and Education after September 11. *Comparative Education, 40*(2), 157-171.

——— (2009, October). *Global Trends in International Student Mobility*. Hong Kong University.

Rizvi, F., & Lingard, B. (2000). Globalization and Education: Complexities and Contingencies. *Educational Theory, 50*(4).

——— (2006). Globalization and the Changing Roles of the OECD's Educational Work. In P. Lauder, P. Brown, J. Dillabough, & A. H. Halsey (Eds.), *Education, Globalization, and Social Change*. New York, NY: Oxford University Press.

——— (2010). *Globalizing Education Policy*. London, UK: Routledge.

Robertson, R. (1990). Mapping the Global Condition: Globalization as the Central Concept. *Theory, Culture & Society, 7*(2), 15-30.

——— (1992). *Globalization: Social Theory and Global Culture*. London, UK: Sage.

Scholte, J. A., & Robertson, R. (2007). *Encyclopedia of Globalization*. New York, NY: Routledge.

Schiller, H., & Phillips, J. D. (Eds.). (1970). *Super-State Readings in the Military-Industrial Complex*. Urbana, IL: University of Illinois Press.

Selingo, J. (2007). Cornell Courts a Subcontinent. *Chronicle of Higher Education, 53*(26).

Shamir, R. (2005). Without Borders? Notes on Globalization as a Mobility Regime. *Sociological Theory, 23*(2), 197-217.

Sidhu, R. K. (2006). *Universities & Globalization: To Market, to Market*. Sociocultural, Political, and Historical Studies in Education. Mahwah, NJ: L. Erlbaum Associates.

Skorton, D. J. (2007). *Globalization of R&D*. Ithaca, NY: Cornell University.

Slaughter, S., & Leslie, L. (1997). *Academic Capitalism: Politics, Policies, and the Entrepreneurial University*. Baltimore, MD: Johns Hopkins University Press.

Spring, J. (2008). Research on Globalization and Education. *Review of Educational Research, 78*(2), 330-363.

Stake, R.E. (1995). *The Art of Case Study Research*. London, UK: Sage.

Tan, S. (2010). Singapore's Educational Reforms: The case for un-standardizing curriculum and reducing testing. *Journal of Scholarship & Practice*. 3(3). Retrieved online from https://www.aasa.org/uploadedFiles/Publications/Journals/AASA_Journal_of_Scholarship_and_Practice/Winter_10%20FINAL%203.pdf#page=50.

Thelin, J. R. (2004). *A History of American Higher Education*. Baltimore, MD: The John Hopkins University Press.

Thompson, G. (2003). *Between Hierarchies and Markets: The Logic and Limits of Network Forms of Organization*. Oxford, UK: Oxford University Press.

Tirman, J. (Ed.). (1984). *The Militarization of High Technology*. Cambridge, UK: Ballinger.

Tudge, C. (2004, Part 804). The Corruption of Science: Mourn for the Honest of Our Most Precious Discipline. *New Statesman*, 29-31.

Uphoff, E. (1991). *Intellectual Property and US Relations with Indonesia, Malaysia, Singapore, and Thailand*. Ithaca NY: SEAP Cornell University.

Van Dijk, J. A. (1999). The One-Dimensional Network Society of Manuel Castells. *New Media & Society, 1*(1), 127-138.

Weiss, L. (1998). *The Myth of the Powerless State*. Ithaca, NY: Cornell University Press.

Weiss, R.S. (1994). *Learning from Strangers: The Art and Method of Qualitative Interview Studies*. New York, NY: Free Press.

Wiley, D., & Root, C. (2003). Educational Partnerships with Foreign Institutions for Increasing the Quality of International Education in the United States. In *Global Challenges and U.S. Higher Education*. Duke University. Retrieved from http://www.jhfc.duke.edu/ducis/globalchallenges/research_papers.html.

William, E. (2007, August 31). Universities Target Foreign Students. *The Times (London)*, 7.

Witt, M.A. (2008). Closed Borders and Closed Minds: Immigration Policy Changes after 9/11 and US Higher Education. *Journal of Educational Controversy*. (3)1. Retrieved online from http://www.wce.wwu.edu/Resources/CEP/eJournal/v003n001/a020.shtml.

Yee, A. H. (Ed.). (1995). Malaysian and Singaporean Higher Education: Common Roots but Differing Directions. In *East Asian Higher Education: Traditions and Transformations*. New York, NY: Pergamon.

Yin, R. K. (1981). The Case Study Crisis: Some Answers. *Administrative Science Quarterly*, 26(1), 58-65.

Young, J. (2010). Singapore's Newest University Is an Education Lab for Technology. *Chronicle of Higher Education*. November 28, 2010. Retrieved online from http://chronicle.com.

Zakaria, F. (2008). *The Post-American World*. New York, NY: W.W. Norton.

Ziman, J. (1994). *Prometheus Bound: Science in a Dynamic Steady State*. New York, NY: Cambridge University Press.

GLOBAL STUDIES IN EDUCATION

A.C. (Tina) Besley, Michael A. Peters,
Cameron McCarthy, Fazal Rizvi
General Editors

Global Studies in Education is a book series that addresses the implications of the powerful dynamics associated with globalization for re-conceptualizing educational theory, policy and practice. The general orientation of the series is interdisciplinary. It welcomes conceptual, empirical and critical studies that explore the dynamics of the rapidly changing global processes, connectivities and imagination, and how these are reshaping issues of knowledge creation and management and economic and political institutions, leading to new social identities and cultural formations associated with education.

We are particularly interested in manuscripts that offer: a) new theoretical, and methodological, approaches to the study of globalization and its impact on education; b) ethnographic case studies or textual/discourse based analyses that examine the cultural identity experiences of youth and educators inside and outside of educational institutions; c) studies of education policy processes that address the impact and operation of global agencies and networks; d) analyses of the nature and scope of transnational flows of capital, people and ideas and how these are affecting educational processes; e) studies of shifts in knowledge and media formations, and how these point to new conceptions of educational processes; f) exploration of global economic, social and educational inequalities and social movements promoting ethical renewal.

For additional information about this series or for the submission of manuscripts, please contact one of the series editors:

A.C. (Tina) Besley:	tbesley@illinois.edu	Department of Educational Policy Studies
Cameron McCarthy:	cmccart1@illinois.edu	University of Illinois at Urbana-Champaign
Michael A. Peters:	mpet001@illinois.edu	1310 South Sixth Street
Fazal Rizvi:	frizvi@unimelb.edu.au	Champaign, IL 61820 USA

To order other books in this series, please contact our Customer Service Department:

(800) 770-LANG (within the U.S.)
(212) 647-7706 (outside the U.S.)
(212) 647-7707 FAX

Or browse online by series:
www.peterlang.com